ONE MAN'S FAITH

ONE MAN'S FAITH

Frank Longford

HODDER AND STOUGHTON
LONDON SYDNEY AUCKLAND TORONTO

For Elizabeth

Scripture quotations are taken from the
Revised Standard Version of the Bible
except where otherwise noted.

British Library Cataloguing in Publication Data

Longford, Frank Pakenham, *Earl of*
 One man's faith.—(Hodder Christian
 paperback)
 1. Christian life
 I. Title
 248.4   BV4501.2

 ISBN 0 340 35989 7

Acknowledgments

I have been indebted to so many friends and so many writers over so many years that I cannot begin to express my gratitude to all those who have, consciously or unconsciously, helped me to write this short book. As always, Elizabeth has been my main inspiration. Then come Gwen Keeble, my long time personal assistant, Barbara Winch, Kitty Chapman and Matthew Oliver, who have all, in one way or another, enabled me to produce the manuscript.

I cannot refrain from mentioning Father Docherty, our former parish priest, Father Maxwell, our present parish priest, at Hurst Green, and Bishop Murphy O'Connor, our Diocesan Bishop. Also Donald Soper, Dick Nugent, Martin Ingleby, John Hunt (of Everest) and Miles Norfolk, Christian leaders in the House of Lords.

Frank Longford

Contents

PART ONE

The Foundations of Belief

1   Personal Narrative

Christianity did not begin for me with my reception into the Catholic Church in 1940 at the age of thirty-four. I was brought up as a Protestant to say my prayers, night and morning. That practice at least I have maintained and indeed, in recent years, somewhat expanded. An undemonstrative undoctrinal Christianity was taken for granted in our family. So was a certain sense of public duty, in no way related to politics. My father was killed leading his brigade at Gallipoli when I was nine. An uncle who did much to take his place lived for fifty years in the East End of London and presided over the largest boys' club in the country. I enjoyed the various games I played there too much for them to be dignified by the name of social work. Half a century later I started, with others, the New Horizon Youth Centre, which is now visited by up to 3,000 young people a year.

At Eton I was about as religious as the average boy. Dr. Alington, the headmaster, supplied me with far more spiritual strengthening than I realised at the time. During the whole of the period when I was an undergraduate I cannot remember going to church on a single occasion, although I may have attended New College Chapel occasionally as an alternative to roll-call. The time came in 1938 when I could no longer resist the psychological imperative to work out a religious position. Two years earlier, when I joined the Labour Party, I had announced, "I am a socialist because I am a Christian," but it was a fairly flimsy claim. I turned to an admired friend, the famous Jesuit Father

Martin D'Arcy. He was Master of Campion Hall, which lay within a stone's throw of Christ Church where I was a "student" (fellow and tutor). From 1938 to 1940 I studied theology amateurishly but more intensively than ever before or since. Meanwhile I was becoming frenetically active in local politics and facing, as we all were, the horrible prospect of the approaching war.

All my life I have been proud to call myself an Irishman. Our family home, now in the possession of my eldest son, remains in County Westmeath. During the 1930s, under the influence of my elder brother (Protestant) and Mr. de Valera (Catholic), the most profoundly religious of modern statesmen, I became an ardent Irish nationalist. This, looking back, seems to me to have affected my attitude to all sorts of questions much more than I realised at the time.

In 1940 I was received into the Catholic Church, as mentioned above. I had satisfied myself at that time that Jesus Christ was crucified and rose again; that he had founded what is now the Catholic Church and had inspired it ever since that time. Certainly I had ceased to be an Anglican and had become a Roman Catholic. The significant fact, however, was that for the first time I had become a systematic and serious-minded Christian. Soon after I was received into the Catholic Church I was invalided out of the Army with a nervous breakdown. I began the war as a private in the infantry and ended it as a private in the Home Guard. It was all very painful at the time, especially to my wife, but there were valuable lessons. Whenever I have tried to be of assistance to failed human beings in the last forty years, I have at least been able to look them in the face and say, "I also have been humiliated."

I worked for three years as personal assistant to Sir William (later Lord) Beveridge, father of the Welfare State. His plan to abolish extreme want – a task so largely accomplished in England, though certainly not in the Third World – carried my fanatical loyalty. I was quite discon-

certed when he was at the height of his fame and I entered a
Catholic church one Sunday to be greeted with the words in
a sermon: "Beveridge is not enough." It was just as well
that I was reminded at that moment of the supremacy of the
spiritual.

Elizabeth, my wife, had been horrified when I was
received into the Catholic Church in 1940. I was in poor
health at the time after my breakdown in the Army and
could not bring myself to tell her for some little time
afterwards. Her antipathy to the Catholic Church had a
triple origin. She had been brought up in a strict Unitarian
household. She had discarded their beliefs but a substra-
tum of anti-Catholicism remained. She was at the centre of
a brilliant sceptical humanist world in Oxford. She had
been for some years an ardent socialist and indeed had had
much to do with my political conversion. In the late 1930s,
left-wing activists identified Catholicism with Franco and
the wicked side in the Spanish Civil War and with reaction
everywhere.

The war went on for five more years. I was in London
much of the time. When she heard of air raids she found
herself praying for me. As our children accumulated (six by
the end of the war), she felt more and more unhappy to see
me going off to my church alone. She had wonderful help
from the Anglican clergy, who were plentiful in Oxford,
and was confirmed in Christ Church Cathedral. Elizabeth
was "received" in February 1946.

The Bishop who had confirmed her as an Anglican
wrote:

> I have no hesitation in thinking that you are doing the only wise
> and right thing. I am certain that, whilst a family that has no
> religion is the worst thing of all, a family of divided allegiances
> is in itself unnatural; and where the division is between father
> and mother the effect on the children is at best unsettling, and
> at worst it goes far to undermine their faith. So I rejoice that
> you are both to walk along the same path (with, I hope, the
> children too), even though it is not the same as mine. I shall

remember you all at Holy Communion as occasion offers; and can assure you of my prayers.

Bearing in mind the ineffable kindness of the Bishop, and of so many other Anglican friends in Christ Church and elsewhere to whom the end of the story must have seemed very plain from the beginning, the debt that Elizabeth and I owe to the Church of England is one we shall never be able to repay.

Evelyn Waugh wrote to her:

> Please let me join the Saints and Angels in their chorus of welcome . . . I do not think anyone outside the Church can ever understand the meaning of the Household of the Faith – the supernatural unity in love that exists behind the superficial wrangles . . . The love within the community is enormously strong and unemotional. It is a fragment of that love I send you today.

Eight children and twenty-two grandchildren have emerged as baptised Catholics, though one of our daughters was tragically killed. They have been a source of unending pride and joy to my wife and myself. We have every reason to offer up prayers of unstinted gratitude.

It is sometimes said that Elizabeth brought me into the Labour Party and that I brought her into the Catholic Church, but the first statement would be much nearer the truth than the second, if only because the hand of God was much less obvious. It is only recently that I have come to realise the enormous part she played even at the time she was not a Christian in preparing me for a true Christianity. It was through her that I came to obtain the beginnings of a perception of the equal worth of all human beings, an essential preliminary to seeing them as all children of the one God, all equally redeemed by Christ.

A few facts about my subsequent life may help to put what follows into context. I was a member of the Attlee Government, though still outside the Cabinet, from 1945 to 1951. I was a member of the Wilson Cabinet and Leader of the House of Lords from 1964 to 1968, resigning on an educational issue. Between my two periods in government I was chairman for eight years of the National Bank. In 1970 I became chairman of the publishers Sidgwick and Jackson, and after ten years in the chair I am now an ordinary director. I have been much involved with social questions, as will appear from subsequent chapters, and have spoken frequently on them and other issues in the House of Lords. I am probably still best known to the general public as an anti-pornographer, but I have devoted much more time and energy to trying to help the disadvantaged and the outcasts. Above all I have persisted in my interest in prisoners, about whom I shall have a good deal to say later on.

"Hate the sin but love the sinner" has been my supreme guideline; the phrase comes, I am told, from Saint Augustine. I have always been conscious that it is not sufficient for Christians to condemn wrongdoing; they must never cease to ask themselves, "What am I doing to help the wrongdoer to avoid the way of transgression?"

Since I left the Cabinet in 1968 I have published short books on *Humility*, on *Jesus Christ* and on *St Francis of Assisi*, in addition to a number of secular works. At the request of the Catholic Church in England I also wrote a life of Pope John Paul II, which appeared at the time of his visit.

It is time to turn from personal narrative to the ultimate issues. Before doing so I should perhaps answer, or rather fail to answer, the question which I honestly do not think can be answered: "What difference has being a Catholic, or what I have called a serious-minded Christian, made to my conduct?" I doubt if leading Christians in public life, like Lord Halifax or Sir Stafford Cripps in the past or Lord Hailsham and Lord Tonypandy (George Thomas) today, could answer that question about themselves. In my case, no one but God could answer the question satisfactorily unless it be Elizabeth, but the first reply will not be available (I hope) for a little while, nor is the second likely to be forthcoming. Anyone who works his way through this book will be equipped to arrive at an answer. I can only hope that he or she will not judge the message by the messenger.

2 Belief in Christ

Today hundreds of millions throughout the world are followers of Christ. He was born in or around 6 BC and crucified in or around April AD 30. He rose from the dead, so Christians believe, on the third day after his crucifixion and, forty days later, ascended into heaven. No human being has ever influenced world history so profoundly. But Christians believe he was not just a human being. They insist that he was at once man and God.

This duality in Jesus Christ's nature sets him apart from any other religious leader. Many millions follow the teachings of Buddha, Mahomet and others. None of these leaders ever claimed divinity.

Jesus was a Jew, a member of a people whose qualities and history were equally exceptional. They were sustained by a conviction that, 2,000 years earlier, God had made a promise to their ancestor Abraham, since then repeatedly renewed. He had undertaken to treat them as his chosen people. The Old Testament is, in the Christian view, a collection of divinely inspired writings concerning God's relations with the people of Israel. The New Testament is concerned with Christ and Christianity. The Old Testament provides the indispensable background for an understanding of the Christian mind.

The distinguished Jewish professor Geza Vermes, who does not recognise Jesus as God in the Christian sense, sees him rather as one of the venerable company of the devout, the ancient Hasidim. "But as compared with the other members of that company," he boldly states, "no objective

and enlightened student of the Gospels can help but be
struck by the incomparable superiority of Jesus." He
quotes another and earlier Jewish authority: "In his ethical
code there is a sublimity, distinctiveness, and originality
in form unparalleled in any other Hebrew ethical code;
neither is there any parallel to the remarkable art of his
parables."

Be that as it may, for over thirty years Jesus Christ lived
on earth as a human being. He ate, drank and slept as other
humans. He experienced human emotions – anger, sorrow
and affection. His body was subject to human frailties,
physical and emotional. In anticipation of his crucifixion he
experienced extreme mental anguish. He died in the most
appalling physical agony.

For the purpose of discussion one must distinguish between the life story, the ethical teaching and the theological
claims of Jesus Christ – though, in fact, they are inextricably interwoven. Christ was a wonder-worker, a sublime
healer. To the leper who said, "If you will you can make me
clean," Jesus said, "I will; be clean" (Lk 5:12–13). To the
paralytic he said, "Take up your pallet and go home,"
having already told him, "Your sins are forgiven" (Mk
2:5, 11). To the woman who had a flow of blood for twelve
years he said, "Daughter, your faith has made you well; go
in peace and be healed of your disease" (Mk 5:34). And so
it was on far more occasions, one surmises, than are
mentioned by the Evangelists.

His ethical teaching will be discussed in Part Two. It is
not set out in academic fashion. Perhaps the most famous
passages of all were delivered in what we know as the
Sermon on the Mount.

Blessed are the poor in spirit, for theirs is the kingdom of
    heaven.
Blessed are those who mourn, for they shall be comforted.
Blessed are the meek, for they shall inherit the earth.
Blessed are those who hunger and thirst for righteousness, for
    they shall be satisfied.

Blessed are the merciful, for they shall obtain mercy.
Blessed are the pure in heart, for they shall see God.
Blessed are the peacemakers, for they shall be called sons of
    God.
Blessed are those who are persecuted for righteousness' sake,
    for theirs is the kingdom of heaven. (Mt 5:3–10)

If only four chapters could be rescued from the entire
New Testament surely they should be John 14 to 17, at the
end of which is his prayer for the disciples with the trium-
phant message: "I made known to them thy name, and I
will make it known, that the love with which thou hast
loved me may be in them, and I in them." (Jn 17:26) But if I
could have only one chapter with me on a desert island it
would be Matthew 18. Humility, tenderness, forgiveness –
all are placed before us there.

There is plenty of room for honest argument about the
miraculous elements in the story and the supernatural
aspect of the claims. In my years of intensive study I devote
much earnest attention to the Resurrection. My conviction
that the Resurrection did indeed occur was crucial to my
renewed Christianity. No one has summed up the whole
issue better than Sir Norman Anderson. Several of his
sentences can be quoted here.

> There is reliable testimony that the Tomb was empty. A large
> number of witnesses attested that Jesus appeared to them after
> His death. The lives of the original disciples changed dramati-
> cally from that point (and led them into heroic courses). The
> Christian Church has borne witness to the same faith all down
> the centuries.

Anderson goes on to point out that St Paul must have
received an outline of it some two to five years after the
Crucifixion itself. Those who insist dogmatically that the
Resurrection *could not* have occurred are flying in the face
of historical evidence. Once the Resurrection is accepted,
the other miraculous features of Christ's life need cause us
no special trouble.

The most remarkable book of Christian apologetics that has come my way in recent years is called *The Way the World Is – the Christian Perspective of a Scientist*. It is by the Rev. John Polkinghorne, FRS. He was until 1979 professor of mathematical physics in the University of Cambridge, a position which he resigned in order to train for the Anglican ministry. He has the distinction of being currently the only Fellow of the Royal Society in holy orders. He, if anyone, must be deemed to bring a truly scientific mind to bear on the truth or otherwise of Christianity.

Chapter 5 in his book is called "The New Testament Evidence". There he writes:

> The kinds of consideration outlined in the preceding chapters would, I think, incline me to take a theistic view of the world. By themselves that is about as far as they would get me. The reason why I take my stand within the Christian community lies in certain events which took place in Palestine two thousand years ago.

He admits that "that in itself is a very odd thing to say." But he insists repeatedly throughout this book that "the experience of science should make one open to the unexpected, aware that apparently slight circumstances may be fraught with large significance. The odd behaviour of a culture near an open window leads to the discovery of penicillin . . ." His examination of the New Testament evidence proceeds along lines not greatly different from those which have led me to my own Christian convictions. He devotes a whole chapter to the Resurrection, where he concludes:

> I believe that the only explanation which is commensurate with the phenomena is that Jesus rose from the dead in such a fashion (whatever that may be) that it is true to say that he is alive today; glorified and exalted but still continuously related in a mysterious but real way with the historical figure who lived and died in first-century Palestine.

In this scientific age it is reassuring to find once again a great man of science combing through all the evidence and reaching the same basic conclusions as those arrived at by countless millions of persons of simple faith. He is very cogent on the subject of miracles. The problem of miracles, he says, is the problem of finding that wider framework in which they can find a coherent place. The relationship of God to his Creation must be faithful and consistent if it is to be in accord with his eternal nature.

But consistency, Rev. Polkinghorne states, does not mean superficial uniformity. "The laws of physics are the same in superconducting and in ordinary regimes, though the consequences are spectacularly different." He points out the claim of the New Testament that in Jesus a totally new regime entered the realm of human experience. If that is the case then in his view it is to be expected that it might be accompanied by new phenomena.

Christian theologians have propounded a variety of views regarding the nature of the divinity of Christ. To deny that divinity altogether places one outside Christianity as I understand it. My own formulation of it makes no claim to originality. It has been expounded times without number but never better in recent times than in *Jesus Then and Now*, by the late David Watson assisted by Simon Jenkins. David Watson quotes many of the most famous sayings, including these:

I am the bread of life; he who comes to me shall not hunger, and he who believes in me shall never thirst (Jn 6:35) . . . I am the light of the world; he who follows me will not walk in darkness, but will have the light of life (Jn 8:12) . . . I am the good shepherd; I know my own and my own know me, as the Father knows me and I know the Father; and I lay down my life for the sheep (Jn 10:14–15). I am the resurrection and the life; he who believes in me will live, even though he die . . . whoever lives and believes in me shall never die (Jn 11:25–26). I am the way and the truth and the life; no one comes to the Father, but by me (Jn 14:6). I am the vine, you are the branches. He who abides in me, and I in him, he it is that bears much fruit, for apart from me you can do nothing (Jn 15:5). I am in the Father and the Father in me (Jn 14:11).

I conclude with Watson and many others that no one could make the claims that Jesus made unless either he were insane or, alternatively, they were true. Yet it is conceded that the ethics of Jesus were the noblest product of the human mind. His healing and caring for the sick illustrated the beauty of his character. The idea that he was insane is itself insane. There is no escaping the conclusion that what he said about himself was true and, accepting that testimony, we must acknowledge that he was divine.

It is appropriate here to quote from an evangelist of an older generation than that of Watson. John Stott was rector of All Souls, Langham Place, from 1950 to 1975 and since then has been rector emeritus. His fame is worldwide. He calls a small book, *Focus on Christ*, an inquiry into the theology of prepositions. We pray to God *through* Christ our mediator. The Church, according to St Paul, is built *upon* the foundations of the Apostles and the Prophets, Christ himself being the cornerstone. To be *in* Christ is to be united to him in a very close personal relationship. Once the objective truth of the God-given supremacy of Jesus has been acknowledged, it is right that we should bow down before him – that we should be *under* Christ our Lord. To be *with* Christ is to share in the four major events of his whole saving career – his death, resurrection, ascension and return . . . If we live, we live *to* the Lord and if we die we die *to* the Lord. The cross of Christ was undertaken *for* us. The Christian mission must be undertaken *for* him – *for* Christ our lover. "Be imitators of me as I am of Christ," wrote the Apostle Paul to early Christian communities. God's whole purpose, writes Stott, may be encapsulated in this single concept. God intends to make us *like* Christ.

However precisely we interpret the incarnation, there is

bound to remain an aura of mystery. The same is, for most of us, still more true of various doctrines which are integral to Christian belief.

Many Christians are fortunate enough to see all these matters in a clear light. Others will fall back on the authority of their Church. They will already have satisfied themselves of the validity of the latter's claims, as I myself did in the case of the Catholic Church over forty years ago. Subsequent events and experiences have served to fortify the convictions then arrived at. I tremble to think of the number of religious books I have read since that time. I must believe that my Christian understanding has been widened and deepened.

To avoid misunderstanding now and later, I must remove any impression that to call a doctrine "mysterious" implies that it is irrational. It may be beyond the power of human thought and expression to set out fully, but it is part of a coherent philosophy and never contrary to logical process. Some of the greatest minds, and some of the simplest, have held these beliefs with equal conviction.

What of the most fundamental question of all, the existence of God? When I was pursuing so fervently my theological studies in the late 1930s, I was a young don passionately concerned to satisfy myself about the rational and argumentative claims of any doctrine I subscribed to. I was impressed, for example, by the apologetic style of Arnold Lunn in his dialogues with C. E. M. Joad, who later himself became a Christian. I remember Martin D'Arcy telling me that Cyril Joad once approached him during the interval in a concert. "Tell me, Father," he said, "can you remind me of St Thomas's fourth proof of the existence of God?" That story seems curiously dated.

In the last forty years, I doubt whether many have been led to a belief in God as a direct result of St Thomas's five proofs. Those proofs have undoubtedly strengthened belief, but the belief itself has originated through many different channels, throughout the centuries and today.

Sometimes it seems to have arisen from the experience of life, sometimes through witnessing the Christian lives of others, sometimes through the arts, especially music, sometimes through nature, and sometimes, as far as one can judge, through divine intervention. For the Rev. Prof. Polkinghorne, the great scientist, as we have seen, it was the Christian story which proved decisive.

C. S. Lewis has carried conviction to many minds in basing a strong proof for the existence of God on "a law of nature of decent behaviour known to all men". Father D'Arcy followed Newman in a subtle and far-ranging argument in favour of the "illative sense". Newman coined the expression to describe "the act of assent in the mind based upon a body of grounds in their totality". The mind might not be aware of all the grounds treated as separate arguments, and might be resting on half-inarticulate experience as well as argument. This was the assent which turned the accumulation of probabilities into certitude.

And why do I personally believe in God? C. S. Lewis, Father D'Arcy and Cardinal Newman have provided me with all the theoretical background needed. Experience of life and the act of faith have done the rest. In my experience the two strongest impediments to Christian belief have been the fact of widespread innocent suffering and the difficulty of accepting the unique claims of Christianity in the light of other religions. The next two sections will therefore be devoted to suffering and comparative religion.

To omit, however, all reference to prayer would seem positively furtive or at least an impression of such complete failure that other parts of the book might be undervalued. In fact I am an old praying hand. I can remember saying my prayers at my mother's knee as far back as I can remember anything. Which takes me back well over seventy years. All that time I have said my prayers twice daily, more recently four times daily, with prayers offered in church as an additional bonus. And I have never at any time been beset by doubts as to whether prayer was worth while.

Everyone is familiar with the teasing questions that can be raised about prayers of petition for oneself or intercession for others. I content myself with the conviction that, if one places oneself in the presence of God and tries to the best of one's ability to accept his will, one's prayers will be answered, though not necessarily in the way that one submits them. I believe that God will never fail to make use of the love offered up in this way in prayer.

But when we come to prayers of thankfulness and praise, when we read of the unremitting efforts by the spiritual masters, male and female, to draw closer to God, we must turn to the masters themselves. I will draw on one of them: St Augustine of Hippo. In his confessions, Augustine describes how, in his Manichean days, he longed for the truth: "Oh my supreme and good Father, Beauty of all things Beautiful. O Truth, Truth, how inwardly did the very marrow of my soul pant for you. Yet all the time you were more inward than the most inward place of my heart and loftier than the highest."

Later he writes that there takes place in prayer "a turning of the heart to him who is always ready to give (his light) if we accept what he gives. In this turning the interior eye is purified with the exclusion of the desire of temporal things."

Almost at random I take this passage from St Francis de Sales:

> I specially recommend mental prayer, and the prayer of the heart, in particular meditation on the life and passion of our Lord; by often looking upon him, your soul will be filled with him, you will understand the dispositions of his heart and model your actions upon his . . . Let us always remain close to him, Philothea, for it is certain we cannot reach God the Father except through this door . . .

The line between adoration and petition or intercession cannot be long sustained. To quote from my favourite psalm, the *Miserere*:

The sacrifice acceptable to God is a broken spirit; a broken and contrite heart, O God, thou wilt not despise.

Do good to Zion in thy good pleasure; rebuild the walls of Jerusalem (Ps 51:17–18).

3   Comparative Religion

Christians today have less reason to be nervous of comparative religion than seemed likely some years ago. I was early aware that comparative religion was a dangerous subject. One of my closest friends was Evan Durbin, a Baptist lay preacher. When he was at New College with me, he lost his Christian faith. Reading Frazer's *The Golden Bough* had done the decisive damage. It seemed to place Christianity on a par with many other religions. And certainly it would be difficult to call oneself a Christian unless one accepted the uniqueness of Christianity, in the sense that it makes unparalleled claims. This would be true of whatever denomination one adhered to.

In recent years I have found the best discussion of the whole subject in Prof. Anderson's *Christianity and Comparative Religion*. By the time I became a Catholic (1940), I had attained a rough grasp of the main points later to be made with such effect by Anderson.

Anderson's sections are headed: "A Unique Proclamation", "A Unique Salvation", "A Unique Disclosure". The fundamental fact about the Incarnation is that it was a *unique* historical event, in which God Himself intervened decisively in the world He had created. The basic difference between Christianity and the mystery religions is the historical basis of the one and the mythological character of the others. We find the same tendency to mythology rather than history in Hinduism.

In Buddhism we have the historical fact of Gautama forsaking the luxurious life of a young Kshatriya prince, and even his sleeping wife and infant son, first for the traditional discipline of the ascetic life and then for solitary meditation – followed, in due course, by his "Enlightenment". But Buddha himself disavowed at the time of his death any divine claims to be made on his behalf. There was certainly no once-and-for-all redeeming event.

Islam is a religion which is clearly historical, but Prof. Anderson, a leading authority on Islamic law and culture, points out the enormous difference between Islam and Christianity. Mohammed was regarded as God's inspired prophet, but not in any sense divine. To the Muslim, it is the divine revelation of which Mohammed was the mouthpiece, rather than any historical event, which is all-important.

Judaism was another historical and nobly monotheistic religion, but the majority of the Jews rejected their Messiah when he came. They failed to recognise the unique historical event when it occurred. The uniqueness of their religion (see below) was of a different kind.

What is the significance of the Christian claim that their message is unique? It helps to confirm the veracity of the Christian story by refuting the argument that the same story can be found in essentials in a number of other religions. It was this argument which weighed so heavily with my friend Evan Durbin and helped to undermine his faith.

But the very uniqueness of Christianity leaves the Christian with a problem whose solution is likely to elude us indefinitely. The Christian claim is naturally offensive to the adherents of every other religious system. It is almost as offensive to modern man – brought up in the atmosphere of relativism, in which tolerance is regarded as perhaps the highest of the virtues.

However, the Christian cannot whittle down his claim to uniqueness. How is he then to regard non-Christians and, in particular, those who believe that they have found their spiritual destiny through other faiths? Many answers have been given to these questions. I myself believe firmly that God intends that all men and women will eventually be saved. But in that case, how can the countless millions be saved through the propitiation of a Saviour of whom they have never heard or whose claims they may have rejected?

For me, it is a firm article of belief, endorsed by the Churches today, that this indeed occurs. But I do not venture an opinion as to how exactly it happens. This is one of the considerable number of mysteries which will not presumably be cleared up in the present life.

It is one thing to claim the uniqueness of Christianity, and another to assert its ethical and spiritual superiority. A Christian, believing as he does that Christ was divine, will inevitably believe that the code he propounded was more elevated than any other. This book is being written by someone who was brought up as a Christian in a country where the overwhelming majority of the population are either Christians or agnostics, or something in between. Even allowing for the influx of Muslims, the question of whether or not to remain a Christian in Britain today is seldom complicated by the claims of rival faiths.

The Jews are in every sense a special case. There were two Jews in a Labour Cabinet. There are three Jews in a Conservative Cabinet at the time of writing. Though they are only one per cent of the population, they have made, and are making, a remarkable contribution to British life in all its aspects. But the question of whether or not to become a Jew arises for hardly anyone in Britain today. I have more than once been privileged to address Jewish audiences and have ventured to remark at the end: "The difference between us is that I would be delighted if you wished to become Christians, you would be horrified if I wished to become a Jew."

Christians are sometimes accused of being exclusive, but the contrast between Christian and Jewish exclusiveness is plain enough. The Jewish religion is linked to a particular people, selected by God as Christians admiringly acknowledge. The Christian religion, in all its uniqueness, is universal in the sense of opening its arms to the world.

What of the Old Testament values? No one who reads the Psalms daily as I do, in the morning and evening prayers, can be unaware of the moral beauties to be found there and in many other parts of the Old Testament. We read in Leviticus 19, "You shall love your neighbour as yourself" (v.18), and a little later, "The stranger who sojourns with you shall be to you as the native among you, and you shall love him as yourself" (v.34). But Exodus 21 lays down the rule, "Eye for eye, tooth for tooth, hand for hand, foot for foot" (v.24), and, "Whoever curses his father or his mother shall be put to death" (v.17).

Beyond all question, the New Testament taken as a whole represents an immense spiritual advance on the Old. On the other hand, the thinking of the best Jewish theologians has progressed far beyond the Pentateuch. The Jews remain *sui generis*, honoured by all Christians who know the history of their own religion. A genuine Christian can never forget the appalling wrongs inflicted by Christians and others on the Jews throughout the centuries. He must redouble his efforts to promote friendship between the two historical communities, who both, to quote Lord Weidenfeld in a notable address, "cherish the heritage of the Bible and are united in their unshakeable loyalty to the Lord who is their common king". More than ninety per cent of Englishmen today would consider the choice to lie between Christianity or some form of humanism, or nothing. Nearly all Christians, if asked which other religion attracted them most, would probably say "Buddhism". It seems necessary, therefore, to dwell on that religion for a moment.

All of us amateur students owe much to the late Judge Christmas Humphreys. He is the first to point out the difficulty of summarising its teaching. "Buddhism", he writes, "may be compared to a set of principles, life tendencies not in the flow of life, vortices of force or matter." So one must not expect to grasp it firmly. The largest distinction in Buddhism today is between the two schools: Theravada Buddhism and Mayahana Buddhism, originally a breakaway movement. There is also Zen Buddhism, associated particularly with Japan.

On the face of it, the conflict between the various schools is sharp. "Much of the teaching to be found today in the Mayahana schools is apparently the exact antithesis of the message as recorded in the Pala canon." So wrote Judge Humphreys, but it did not prevent his drafting twelve principles of Buddhism, which won a wide measure of acceptance throughout the Buddhist world. He writes:

> Life being One, the interests of the part should be those of the whole. In his ignorance, man thinks he can successfully strive for his own interests, and this wrongly-directed energy of selfishness produces suffering. He learns from his suffering to reduce (a) the omnipresence of suffering; (b) its cause, wrongly directed desire; he also learns (c) its cure: the removal of the cause and (d) the Noble Eightfold Path of Self-Development, which leads to the end of suffering.

The Eightfold Path of Self-Development (right aim, right speech, right acts, etc.) could be adopted without difficulty by any well-meaning person, Christian or otherwise, but the Buddhist religion is a religion without God. In addition, it rejects the immortality of the soul.

A Christian who lost his faith in a personal God and immortality might well find in Buddhism a consoling alternative, but reincarnation seems integral to its fundamental teaching and not many of us brought up in the West will find that acceptable. Christmas Humphreys says at the end of one of his books: "The West will never be Buddhist and only the most unthinking zealot would strive to make it so."

Sixty-five years ago my best friend at my preparatory school was called Alan Griffiths. He defeated me in the school boxing final. For many years now he has been Father Bede Griffiths, resident in an ashram in south India. He has lived "as an Indian among Indians, following Indian ways of life, studying Indian thought and immersing himself in the living traditions of the Indian spirit". I have seen him only on television, white robed and white bearded. I am afraid he would not like altogether what I have written above. It would seem dangerously narrow-minded. "The eternal religion," he writes, "is to be found in every religion at its ground or source, but it is beyond all formulation. It is also to be found in the heart of every man. It is the law 'written on their hearts'." But no one can read his book *Return to the Centre* without recognising with him the uniqueness of the Christian revelation.

A few words about Marxism are inevitable in a section concerned with rival faiths, though I would never call Marxism a religion. One of my set books when I was studying at Oxford for the Philosophy, Politics and Economics examination in 1927 was Marx's *Capital*. I went quite deeply into his labour theory of value, though still a Conservative at the time. Throughout the 1930s I was teaching political theory, which included Marx. I also became involved with Communism in practice. When I stood for the Cowley and Iffley ward of Oxford City Council, my colleague on the "slate" was a Communist. I was deeply involved in the United Front in the years leading up to the war. I lectured and organised lectures on most aspects of Marxism.

The main teachings I was concerned with were the class war, the materialist conception of history and dialectical materialism. There was a time when I thought it was possible, absurdly as it now seems to me, to propound a form of Christian Marxism – Christianity, one might say, internally, Marxism externally. That seems pretty good nonsense now, but that was in the days when Russia seemed, and in one sense was, the strongest potential ally against Nazi Germany. Socialists from the Webbs downwards managed to shut their eyes to the wicked totalitarianism of the Communist regime.

Marxism emerging in the horrifying form of Soviet Communism has aroused the same dedicated readiness for sacrifice that we find, for example, in Christianity. But so, during its shorter period of life, did Nazism. If I am asked why I do not allow the title of religion to Communism and Nazism, while allowing it, for example, to Buddhism (though Buddhism, as they do, rejects a personal god), I would say that Communism and Nazism, unlike Buddhism, are concerned only with events in the outer world, not with the personal life. For the Communist, as for the National Socialist, there is no code of personal ethics. Everything, every problem of conduct, is related to the political or social end. I will never ignore the historical angle but never, even during the short period when I toyed with the idea of Christian Marxism, did I expect to find in it a route to personal salvation.

Throughout this chapter I have sought to demonstrate the uniqueness of Christian theology. In the next one I shall be speaking in similar terms of Christian ethics, though in fact Christian theology and Christian ethics can never be separated except for purposes of discussion.

PART TWO

Christian Ethics

4   Christians and Non-Christians

Christians believe that their moral code is nobler than any other and that they possess additional sources of grace which are less readily available elsewhere. There are certain passages in C. S. Lewis's brilliant little book *Mere Christianity* which might appear to contradict the first of these statements, but not in the light of what he writes later.

Lewis was very anxious to base a strong proof for the existence of God on "a law of Nature or decent behaviour known to all men . . .". He states:

> There have been differences between different civilisations but these have never amounted to anything like a total difference . . . Men have differed as regards what people you ought to be unselfish to – whether it was only your own family, or your fellow countrymen, or every one. But they have always agreed that you ought not to put yourself first. Selfishness has never been admired. Men have differed as to whether you should have one wife or four. But they have always agreed that you must not simply have any woman you liked.

Later, however, he singles out a number of ways in which Christianity rises superior to other codes. He mentions chastity as the most unpopular of the Christian virtues. A little further on, however, he says this of forgiveness:

> I said in a previous chapter that chastity was the most unpopular of the Christian virtues. But I am not sure I was right. I believe there is one even more unpopular. It is laid down in the

Christian rule: "Thou shalt love thy neighbour as thyself."
Because in Christian morals "thy neighbour" includes "thine
enemy", and so we come up against this terrible duty of
forgiving our enemies.

Further on again he seems to displace both chastity and
forgiveness from the position of the supreme Christian
virtue. He comes to what he calls "the great sin": on this he
writes:

> I now come to that part of Christian morals where they differ
> most sharply from all other morals. The vice I am talking of is
> pride or self-conceit and the opposite to it in Christian morals
> is called humility. According to Christian teachers pride leads
> to every other vice.

So C. S. Lewis proves to be a strong champion of the
distinctiveness and the superiority of Christian ethics. This
leads us on inexorably to the next question.

Are Christians really "better" in their conduct than
non-Christians? This is not a question which in my experience Christians are very happy to discuss. To claim any
kind of superiority does not commend them to non-
Christians. They themselves may feel that it is incompatible with Christian humility. It is, moreover, a claim the
truth of which could never be demonstrated scientifically.
Whatever meaning we attach to one kind of conduct being
"better" than another, and however we define "Christians", there could never be a controlled experiment which
compared like with like and reached an irrefutable conclusion.

Nevertheless humility is supposed to involve a recognition of truth, and if Christian believers, leaving out their
personal merits, consider that their fraternity behaves
better on average than those outside it, they ought not to be
ashamed of saying so. Not to mention the point is, indeed,
to deprive themselves of a crucial argument in favour of
their religion. It lays them open to the tiresome question:

"What is the point of your religion if it does not make you behave better than anyone else?"

It surely flies in the face of common sense to suggest that there is no correlation between belief and conduct. Of course, there is always the Evelyn Waugh position. When pressed occasionally to explain why he, a devout Catholic, was not "nicer", he would reply: "You have no idea how nasty I would be if I were not a Catholic." But that is too modest a perspective. Christians believe, as stated above, that their moral code is the most elevated and that they possess additional sources of grace. In my experience they examine their consciences much more systematically than others are inclined to. They have the life of Jesus Christ as a sublime model. It would be strange indeed if their conduct in no way reflected these advantages, if they did not behave any better than the majority of their fellow citizens who lack an ethical code, or those whose ethical code is inferior.

I am not of course saying that *all* Christians are better than *all* non-Christians. Whatever the criterion of virtue adopted, that would be patently ridiculous. I am submitting that *on average* Christians behave better than non-Christians – as indeed they ought to. I am talking about the moral consequences of belief. I am not treating belief itself as a moral virtue. Whether we believe or not depends on so many factors outside our control. Nor am I implying any opinion whatever about the judgment which will be passed on all of us on the last day.

But what, for our present purpose, do I mean by calling someone a Christian? The word is used in various ways, most of them not unflattering to Christianity. I differed acutely over abortion with a good friend of mine in the House of Lords. She, an admitted humanist, shook her finger at me afterwards and insisted: "I'm a better Christian than you are!"

On the way to my office recently, I was stopped by a worker on a building site who demanded: "Why do you want such and such a prisoner released?"

I asked him a little sharply: "Are you a Christian?"
He replied amiably: "Of course I am."
The dialogue went on:
"Do you go to church?"
"No way."
"Do you say your prayers?"
"No way" to that also.
"Then how can you call yourself a Christian?"
"Because I love my neighbour. I've never done a bad thing in my life."
I said: "You must be the only man in the world who hasn't."
We parted on good terms.
A simple test is whether the person, if asked "Are you a Christian?" replies "Yes". But neither that nor any other test is altogether satisfactory. I was once asked by the late Anthony Crosland – sitting next to me in the Cabinet – why, in a speech in the House of Lords I was proposing to describe our Cabinet as Christian. I made a rough count round the table and whispered to him: "Eleven Christians, five non- or anti-Christians, five don't knows." That was, of course, a half-serious speculation, but he seemed to feel that it might be about right. He agreed with me that the three leading members of the Cabinet, Messrs Wilson, Brown and Callaghan, could fairly be labelled Christians. But even if I had had an inconceivable amount of insight into the inner lives of my colleagues, a convincing classification could hardly have been possible.
My real submission may seem complicated but to me, at least, it has high significance, namely that those who deliberately govern their lives according to the religion of Jesus Christ will on average behave better than those who do not. I submit further that the moral performance of such Christians will tend to vary directly with the degree of their devotion. I acknowledge, as one must, the horrors that can result from religious fanaticism. Religious fanatics spoil the

moral average of Christian believers, but do not invalidate the argument.

During the devaluation crisis of 1966, Jim Callaghan, then Chancellor of the Exchequer, told me that he had been brought up in a strict Nonconformist household, but under pressure of public business he had not said his prayers regularly for years. He had just begun to say them again. To the best of my belief he has continued to do so ever since. Of course, I have no evidence for saying that he became a better man after he returned to prayer. But I shall continue to make that supposition.

An ambiguity must be cleared up at once. Am I claiming that Christians are better according to Christian standards, or that they are better by standards broadly accepted by the whole community? I am audacious enough to make both claims. I am confining the comparison to Great Britain – though Ireland, north and south, is not lost sight of.

This means in practice that the comparison is between Christians on the one hand and, on the other (leaving out the Jews) those who in the great majority of cases practise no religion of their own. In a relatively small number of cases they will have worked out a system for themselves, but statistically speaking this would not be common. The impact of eastern religions on the general culture of the country is still insubstantial.

To return to our theme. C. S. Lewis, quoted above, has singled out chastity, forgiveness and humility as distinctive Christian virtues. I will deal with the last two in chapters 6 and 5 respectively. The discussion of chastity leads on to sex and the family and can be more conveniently looked at separately (see Chapter 8).

A few words, however, must first be said about the supreme virtue of charity. Christianity claims first and last to be the religion of love. The parable of the Good Samaritan teaches us to see our neighbour in all men and women, and elsewhere in the Gospels we are taught to love our enemies. It would be presumptuous, and today patently untrue, to claim a Christian monopoly for the doctrine of universal brotherhood, or for women being treated on precisely the same footing as men. The Christian inspiration and explicit injunction to love one another as Christ loved us are, however, uniquely powerful. They are inseparable from his death on the cross for the salvation of us all.

In his *Mere Christianity* C. S. Lewis writes: "Christian love or charity to our neighbours is quite a different thing from liking or affection." He acknowledges, however, that though Christian charity is quite distinct from affection, it leads to affection. Lewis reminds us that some writers use the word "charity" to describe not only Christian love between human beings, but also God's love for man and man's love for God. If we find ourselves failing to love God, there is only one answer – act as though we love him. "The great thing to remember is that, though our feelings come and go, his love for us does not." There is no doubt that, as Solzhenitsyn, among many others, has pointed out, it is vastly easier to love every single human being if we really can see him or her as a child of God.

In a moment I shall be making a wider claim that Christians are on average morally better than non-Christians – even according to standards accepted by everyone, of which unselfishness is an obvious expression. But before I come to that, I am making a still more obvious point. It is inconceivable that those who do not subscribe to Christian doctrines of sexual conduct should practise them as faithfully as those who regard them as binding.

No single example is a proof in itself, but Bertrand Russell, admired for so many reasons, will serve as a good illustration. In various books he propounded a code of morals which won many adherents. It included what used to be called "free love". It is a code full of sinfulness by Christian standards. We must, if we are charitable, love the sinners in question, but we cannot fail to condemn the sin.

The doctrines of free love are not, of course, new. Lord

Russell's second wife wrote a moving, and indeed brilliant, autobiography. She described her own strong opposition to marriage, but when a child was on the way she agreed to marry Bertrand Russell because he so urgently desired an heir to his future earldom. After marriage they persisted in their life of free love. In their case, the marriage was subjected to too many strains and did not endure.

In the dazzling Bloomsbury circle, homosexuality was much more popular than it ever was with Bertrand Russell. But free love was an article of faith. We are all familiar by now with the extraordinary world of Ham Spray. Lytton Strachey was in love with Ralph Partridge. Ralph Partridge was married to Carrington, who was so passionately in love with Lytton Strachey that she committed suicide when he died. Frances Marshall, who has described it all unforgettably, eventually married Ralph Partridge.

Nigel Nicolson, in reviewing a life of Vanessa Bell, sister of Virginia Woolf, quotes with approval a comment of Roger Fry: "It really is almost an ideal family, based as it is on adultery and mutual forbearance, with Clive, the deceived husband, and me, the abandoned lover. It really is rather a triumph of reasonableness over the conventions." As Mr. Baldwin once remarked: "There are many aspects of truth" – and of its opposite. It is all fascinating to read about. We may be disposed to make allowances for genius and some arresting personalities. Lytton Strachey was remarkably kind to me on the only occasion I met him, when I was far out of my depth at a Bloomsbury party on election night, 1931. As a code of life, however, it would be totally destructive of any society that practised it extensively. The Bloomsbury world left few descendants.

Leaving out the sexual component, is non-Christian morality, as ordinarily understood in Britain, inferior to that of Christians? So far I have argued that it ought to be, if Christianity is true. But how can I demonstrate that it is so in practice? I should say at once that I have found it so in my own, somewhat prolonged, experience – a relevant point in a book such as this entitled *One Man's Faith*. But how can one begin to convince those who are reluctant to accept any such proposition?

I am forced to concede that statistics and such like evidence are not in the nature of things available on either side of the argument. I will produce a few examples that weigh with me.

In the autumn of 1983 I attended a conference of the Prison Christian Fellowship in Belfast. Thirty-one nations were represented, though it had been in existence less than ten years. It was created and spread throughout the world by Charles Colson, once President Nixon's hatchet man, who went to prison through his involvement in Watergate. Through the Christian inspiration of some who befriended him in his darkest hour, he became a Born-Again Christian and has provided an as effective a witness to Christ as any man of our period.

On my way to Belfast, I was driven from the airport by another more recently Born-Again Christian – a youngish man recently released from prison, after serving six years for violent offences. He had been a prominent member of the illegal Protestant paramilitary force, the Ulster Volunteer Force, a body as deeply involved in killing as the IRA. He told me that he had been made to share a cell with a one-legged prisoner whom he bullied. This prisoner's attitude was so truly Christian that he himself was converted to a dedicated Christianity. Can one imagine a conversion of this kind to any form of humanism? I hardly think so.

What non-Christian examples can I select with a measure of fairness? The individuals chosen should at least be admired for one reason or another. Let us take the aforementioned Bertrand Russell at his own valuation. In his autobiography, he describes his treatment of a whole number of women, including his four wives. He describes without shame and even with pride an approach which was not only that of a male chauvinist, but consistently callous. Let us agree that he was an intellectual genius and, in some respects, an heroic figure in his readiness to go to prison twice for his beliefs. But his code of personal behaviour compares unfavourably with that of even mediocre Christians.

I will draw my other two examples of humanist morality from two of the outstanding intellectuals of our time – one of them a great friend, the other I was immensely fond of, though I seldom saw him in recent years. Alan (A. J. P.) Taylor has told us in his autobiography that he never forgave his first wife, Margaret, who admittedly tried him hard, or his old friend and patron, Prof. Namier. The latter's attitude to Alan's candidature for the Regius Professorship of history at Oxford seemed to Alan so appalling that he refused Namier's attempt at a reconciliation. A Christian might have failed in forgiveness – Christians often do – but he would never boast of his non-forgiveness.

Arthur Koestler, in his middle seventies, was suffering from a terrible disease. He and his wife deliberately committed suicide as a principled act of euthanasia. Even a severe critic of the action must recognise the depth of love involved. Once again, however, it is inconceivable that a Christian, even if he found life unbearable – and many Christians have committed suicide – would have allowed his much younger wife to join him in this mutual destruction.

How do non-Christians reply to the above line of argument? The late Lord Francis-Williams was an active and articulate humanist and, by any standards, an ethical man. I had the honour of giving an address at his funeral at the invitation of his widow. He tells us in his autobiography of a small dining group which he attended in company with such brilliant intellectuals as A. J. Ayer, Julian Huxley and Barbara Wootton. (The last-named has done more for penal reform in practice than anyone in recent years.) They were anxious to find a form of words to encapsulate the humanist ideal. The best they could manage was "limited certainty", which all agreed was not a great rallying cry.

Except in the negative sense of rejecting God and personal immortality, humanists will always suffer from the absence of a common doctrine. They will say with confidence, however, that Christians are concerned with the demands of an arbitrary God and with an imaginary next world, instead of concentrating on what is best for human beings in this one. They will apply, in effect, a this-worldly utilitarianism. They seek to calculate, by rational means, what provides the greatest happiness *in this life* of the greatest number. Christians should be ready to take them up on their own ground, though their ideas of happiness might differ. Was J. M. Keynes, the supreme economist, happier than Archbishop Temple, a spiritual counterpart?

Beatrice Webb, in the second part of her published Diaries, has nothing but contempt for Benthamism and the crude ideas of happiness associated with the utilitarians. She mentions some of the values in life which meant most to her and for which no room was found for in Benthamism. One is reminded of a sentence in one of Cardinal Newman's *University Sermons*: "The Roman Stoic as he committed suicide complained he had worshipped virtue, and found it but an empty name."

"The Benthamites omitted from their calculations some of the most powerful impulses of human nature: reverence for mystery, admiration for moral beauty, longing for the satisfaction of an established expectation, custom and habit, tradition, sense of honour, sense of humour, passionate longing for truth, loyalty" (Beatrice Webb). She was a humanist with mystical leanings. This chapter has been concerned with virtue, not happiness. I am not arguing here that, in a quantitative sense, there is more or less happiness among Christians than non-Christians, because the kind of happiness in the one case is incommensurable with the kind of happiness in the other.

Be that as it may, Christians should not allow the claims of the next world to be opposed to those in this one. They do not arrive at their ethical conclusions by unassisted human reason. They import "revelation", whose validity they cannot expect humanists to acknowledge. It is part of the Christian task to make sure that reason and revelation finish up in harmony. Not many individual Christians are capable of performing this task on their own. The Churches are indispensable.

But being a Christian is not necessarily a short cut to ease and comfort. The Christian may be beset with spiritual complexities, which arise from his higher moral aspirations, his yearning for spiritual growth. The best Christians will sometimes be troubled in spirit in a fashion of which the humanist knows little. When I was being informally instructed by the great spiritual adviser, Father Martin D'Arcy SJ, I told him of various anxieties of mine and asked whether, if I became a more firmly based Christian, they would disappear. He replied that I must make no such assumption. If the example of the saints was anything to go by, the anxieties would be transferred to a higher plane.

5   Humility

"It would be an error," says Father Canice in his excellent book *Humility* (1951), one of the few books written about humility at any time, "to think that humility is the most excellent of the virtues . . . But insomuch as it is the basis of every virtue, humility is first: from it all the virtues begin, through it they grow. In it they are perfected and by it they are maintained."

But how exactly do we define humility? In my small book, *Humility* (1969), I quoted an encounter with my friend Bishop Stockwood when I was writing it. "Humility, a very elusive subject," said Mervyn Stockwood, turning away hastily when I begged him for a definition of it at a religious cocktail party. Father Corbishley SJ commented at the beginning of his introduction to my book: "Readers of Lord Longford's book may well feel as they come to the end of it that humility is indeed a very elusive subject." At the time of writing, I cannot say otherwise, but I am more insistent than ever that it is, along with forgiveness, the most distinctive of all the Christian qualities.

Christian humility begins with Christ. In a sense it ends there. The Oxford Dictionary of the Christian Church points out that humility is not just a virtue, so to speak, *in vacuo*. It was specifically enjoined by Christ in his teaching and illustrated above all by the example of his life and death.

The whole life and death of Christ can be seen as a stupendous example of the virtue. The point has never been put more effectively than in Philippians 2:6–8:

(Jesus Christ), though he was in the form of God, did not count equality with God a thing to be grasped, but emptied himself, taking the form of a servant, being born in the likeness of men. And being found in human form he humbled himself, and became obedient unto death, even death on a cross.

The whole Gospel story throws light directly or indirectly on humility as divinely interpreted. Our Lord's life begins in the manger, then comes the subjection at Nazareth to his parents; his work as an obscure carpenter; his inflexible pursuit of his Father's will in all his enterprises until his death in agony and humiliation on the cross. In one way or another the message of humility emerges from every section of his teaching, whether to the parable of the Prodigal Son or to the supreme summons: "If any man would come after me, let him deny himself and take up his cross and follow me" (Mk 8:34).

Of the nine Beatitudes, only two are directly concerned with humility: "Blessed are the poor in spirit; blessed are the meek, for they shall inherit the earth" (Mt 5:3,5). The explicit references in the Gospels are not, indeed, very numerous. A few quotations must suffice us here: "Come to me," cried Jesus Christ, "all who labour and are heavy laden, and I will give you rest. Take my yoke upon you and learn from me; for I am gentle and lowly in heart, and you will find rest for your souls. For my yoke is easy, and my burden is light" (Mt 11:28–30).

Putting a child in the midst of them, he said:

Unless you turn and become like children, you will never enter the kingdom of heaven. Whoever humbles himself like this child, he is the greatest in the kingdom of Heaven (Mt 18:3–4) . . . Whoever would be great among you must be your servant, and whoever would be first among you must be slave of all. For the Son of man also came not to be served but to serve, and to give his life as a ransom for many (Mk 10:43–45) . . . He who is greatest among you shall be your servant; whoever exalts himself will be humbled, and whoever humbles himself will be exalted (Mt 23:11–12).

At the Last Supper, he rose and laid his garments aside and began to wash the feet of the disciples. Peter tried to prevent him, but Jesus answered, "If I do not wash you, you have no part in me" (Jn 13:8).

But what is there specifically Christian about humility? I will take an example of the most humble statesman I have known. Lord Attlee's true humility was palpable to anyone who knew him. But one had to know him well to realise that his humility went to the depth of his being. When he ceased to be Prime Minister, he returned to Great Missenden from the House of Lords on the Underground. He travelled second class whenever possible. He could not believe, as I found on a particular occasion, that his cheque would be cashed in a restaurant. He saw himself as "an ordinary bloke", and so he remained to the end.

But for the accident of the Labour Party débâcle in 1931, he would never have become leader of the Labour Party or Prime Minister. Once installed, he remained leader of the Party for twenty years and Prime Minister for six, firmly resisting all attempts to eject him. He was adamant in defence of his rights when they coincided with his duties.

It may be pointed out that he was not, according to his own account, a theological Christian, though no one in my experience of politics exhibited Christian ethics more convincingly. But he was brought up in a strong Christian tradition. He told his biographer that his best friends were usually Christians. His humility can be fairly attributed in no small degree to his Christian formation.

In my small book on humility, I examine a good many non-Christian views on this virtue, including those of scientists and psychologists. It did not seem to me then (1969), nor does it seem to me now, that a Christian view of humility can be readily discovered outside Christianity. It is not difficult to set aside Aristotle. "If the superior man," said Aristotle, "does not condemn the rest of the world, it is with justice, and because he takes a correct view of his relation to it." Not much analogy with Christianity there.

The non-Christian, anxious to prove that the best minds outside Christianity have arrived at humility independently, would find their best illustration, perhaps, in Marcus Aurelius. I gave a number of ways in which Marcus Aurelius expressed a "holier than thou" attitude: "Nobody can implicate me in what is degrading." But it is simpler to point to his repeated conviction that man can perfect himself: "Bear in mind that no man can hinder you from conforming each word and deed to that nature of which you are a part."

The Christian tradition of humility has been proclaimed in ringing tones by nearly all the spiritual leaders. St Augustine could write, *Tota Christiana religio humilitas est* ("The whole of Christian religion is humility."). St Benedict, in his famous rule issued from the solitude of Monte Cassino about AD 535, set forth twelve degrees of humility. He is assured that the monk who had ascended all these degrees of humility would soon arrive at the perfect charity. Thomas à Kempis, in his *Imitation of Christ* (1418), is above all concerned to help us towards a relationship with Christ. It is only when we bear our cross in the spirit of humility, whether it has been imposed on us or whether we have gone to seek it in the service of others, that it draws as close as humans can be to Christ himself.

In the *Introduction to the Devout Life* (1608), St Francis de Sales says of humility: "The saints and above all the King of Saints and His mother have always cherished this virtue above all the other moral virtues." Père de Caussade SJ, who has been so sensitively translated by Kitty Muggeridge, preaches self-abandonment – the "loving acceptance of all that God sends at every moment". The supreme obstacle is revealed as vanity, the accursed passion; without humility there can be no hope of spiritual progress.

Teilhard de Chardin, coming to more recent times, asked himself the question, "How can we reconcile the love of God and the healthy love of the world?" He did not use the word humility but there emerges from Teilhard an analogous doctrine. We must at all stages of our lives sink our personal ambitions in the cooperation with God in all the duties that fall to us. Most notably the duty of accepting our gradual diminishment and passage to death.

Pope John XXIII, when he was twenty-one, wrote down a resolve that he was to follow till death. "The way I must take," he concludes, "is the way of humility. I must go straight along this path and never turn back." To the end of his life he adhered indomitably to his motto "Obedience and Peace". In the last entry of all in his Journal he gives a summary of great graces "bestowed on a man who has a low esteem of himself but receives good inspirations and humbly and trustfully proceeds to put them into practice". In spite of the "success" which he was too honest not to acknowledge, he remained to the end aware that it was God, not he, who had "provided the increase".

Gerald Vann – born 1906, died 1963 – would laugh at the suggestion that he should be placed on a par with the foregoing writers. But in his book *The Divine Pity* he expressed a doctrine of humility which is of supreme relevance to the present time.

> To care and not to care; the courage and strength of the love of the saints in spreading abroad in the world the spirit of love; the meekness and humility of the saints in refusing to be upset by attacks upon themselves; these are the two aspects of a single unified life, the life of humility. To care and not to care: humility can love the whole world because it recognises that the whole world is God's; and it is carefree because it has nothing to lose – not even its own self-respect.

To care and not to care. Humility means having zeal for great works, but always behind the power and ambition there is "Thy will be done". In my book *Humility*, already mentioned, I distinguished five ideas in this Christian virtue: knowledge of oneself as one is; the opposite quality to pride; meekness in conduct; obedience; willingness to serve others. I do not wish to improve on that analysis now.

But I was worried then, and am still worried, by the emphasis laid by so many spiritual writers on humility as truth. In our relationship with God, I see no theoretical difficulty. The humble Christian will recognise his infinite worthlessness and insignificance in relation to God. He will recognise also that it is just as much part of his total situation to be a child of God as it is to be a sinner, and that as a child of God he is infinitely dear to him. It is when we explore this aspect of humility in relation to our fellow human beings that complexities confront us.

I take the following extract almost at random from Walter Hilton's *The Ladder of Perfection* (fourteenth century):

> Honour all men and regard them as your betters, behaving humbly in their company, and seeing yourself as *the most worthless and insignificant of men* [my italics]. It will do you no harm however much you humble yourself, even though in God's sight you have more grace than another. But it is dangerous for you to consider yourself superior to anyone else, even though he may be the most depraved and wicked scoundrel alive.

Surely there is a danger of mock modesty here?

A few words finally on humility as opposed to pride. The official embodiment of pride is Satan himself. It is the worst of the deadly sins, often contrasted with humility, which is sometimes described as the most Christian of the virtues. Pope John's diary has already been mentioned. In the second entry, he wrote, when aged fourteen: "Above all, I will watch myself carefully, lest the tree of pride should grow in me; I will beware of this, keeping myself humble-minded and the lowliest of all, both in pious practices and in study." Sixty-five years later, he heads the last entry of all: "Summary of Great Graces Bestowed on a Man who Thinks Poorly of himself". The contrast between pride and humility, vice and virtue, could hardly be put more sharply.

In ordinary discussion, pride is not always by any means

a term of abuse. Few would deny that there can be such a thing as proper pride. We can take it surely that the Pope is proud of being Polish and Cardinal Hume proud of being a son of Ampleforth. Prince Charles at the time of his wedding said that he was proud of being British. I have said many times that I am proud to call myself an Irishman. But in contrast I refer here to improper pride, more particularly ambition and arrogance. Can we put our finger on what it is in pride which has caused it to be selected as the most evil of all sins?

One way of answering that question is to say that in so far as we suffer from pride, and we all suffer from it to a greater or lesser extent, we are treating ourselves as sacred objects of worship. In the theological sense, we are putting ourselves in the place of God; supplanting God whether or not we believe in Him, and continue to claim that we worship Him. But here we enter into a complicated area. We encounter the whole problem of legitimate and illegitimate egotism. I often find myself returning to the second commandment – that we should love others as we love ourselves, and asking myself, "In what sense should I love myself?" In what sense should anyone love himself? It seems clear from the Gospel instructions that, in some sense, this is an ineluctable duty.

I say all this to prevent an air of unreality surrounding the Christian virtue of humility. An air of unreality, of overdone perfection, must not be allowed to diminish the attractiveness of Christian humility, which – properly understood – should help us to live our lives at all times more abundantly.

Pope John Paul II exhibits, for millions who have seen him and for thousands who have met him, an extraordinary combination of humility and strength. When I was received by him in Rome I could only blurt out the words, "It is very good of you to see me." He replied with extraordinary modesty, "It is very good of you to come to see me." The words were conventional enough, but the way he said them left an ineffaceable impression. What I can only call his gentle diffidence did not for one moment detract from his air of limitless strength.

6   Forgiveness

The doctrine of forgiveness is central to Christianity. Along with humility, forgiveness distinguishes Christian ethics from all other systems. Charity, in one form or another, has been advocated by many religious teachers and philosophers outside Christianity, although we Christians claim to give it a deeper and wider meaning. But in regard to forgiveness, Christianity tells us that God took human form in Jesus Christ, that he showed a special concern for sinners and died on the cross to redeem sinful mankind.

The Gospels are permeated through and through with the idea of forgiveness. When Peter asked Christ, "How often shall my brother sin against me, and I forgive him? As many as seven times?" Jesus replied, "I do not say to you seven times, but seventy times seven" (Mt 18:21–22). In other words, indefinitely. He said to the accusers of the woman taken in adultery, "Let him who is without sin among you be the first to throw a stone" (Jn 8:7). And to the woman herself, "Neither do I condemn you" (Jn 8:11). That last phrase has been used quite often in recent times as a reason for not condemning anything at all, for being, to use the modern jargon, non-judgmental.

We should, however, remember that Christ said to the same woman, "Go and do not sin again" (Jn 8:11). In other words he did not fail to condemn the sin because he loved the sinner. As he hung in agony from the cross, he prayed for his tormentors: "Father, forgive them; for they know not what they do" (Lk 23:34). And to the penitent thief he gave this assurance: "Today you will be with me in Paradise" (Lk 23:43).

Every time a Christian says the Our Father, he uses the words: "Forgive us our trespasses, as we forgive those who trespass against us." In short, Christianity and forgiveness are so wrapped together that they cannot be separated.

We could consider forgiveness either from the theological or from the ethical standpoint; either from the point of view of our relationship to God, or from that of our conduct to our fellow men. But, of course, one cannot really separate the two. As Christians we have a special consciousness of our inherent sinfulness and a conviction, however shadowy, of what it means to be pardoned by God through Jesus Christ. In our attitude to our fellow men, we seek, however feebly, to give effect to those values on our own plane.

But once again it seems to be convenient to subdivide the subject under two main headings. The problem of forgiveness comes home to many of us when we read in the newspapers of some outrageous crime or some deviation (it may be by public men whom we otherwise respect) from normal standards of conduct; or it may come closer home, when we are forced to ask ourselves whether we are capable of forgiving someone who has inflicted a small or large injury, either on ourselves or on those who are dear to us. It may focus our ideas if I examine closely the application of forgiveness to convicted criminals, with whom I happen to have had a large and intimate acquaintanceship over the last forty years.

I start from the assumption that a good Christian is a forgiving person. Though few of us would claim to be good Christians, we are at least ready to try to live up to that standard. But what is meant by forgiveness in general and how do we apply it to convicted criminals?

When I am talking of convicted criminals, I am referring to a great mass of highly various human beings, each of them completely individual. Many of them have committed small crimes, but some have been involved in huge bank robberies, vicious assaults and brutal murders. If I seem to be thinking more of the extreme cases, it is because their position and our treatment of them bring out the nature of the problem in its most acute form. Certainly no theory of forgiveness deserves the name of Christian which does not cater for them.

The problem of punishment cannot be dodged. I assume that no civilised society would be possible if those who flagrantly broke the basic rules were not punished. We can all argue – I spend quite a bit of my time arguing – as to what form those rules should take. We can argue in particular cases whether someone has indeed been rightly found guilty of breaking them. We can argue as to whether imprisonment is the right punishment, and for how long, if imprisonment is imposed at all, it should last. And if we don't like the word punishment, we can go on arguing about that. We can try to find a better word.

But I have never found any serious person who believed that those who commit grave offences should go scot-free. Offences against the law will in fact continue on a greater or lesser scale. Those that commit them must be penalised, over a period perhaps of many years, and a Christian visitor to a prisoner is faced with the question: "How can you pretend that society is forgiving me if it keeps me here in bondage?"

There are, of course, many citizens, including not a few Christians, who do not think that we ought to forgive criminals – at any rate until they have purged their offence, which may be, as I have said, a matter of many years. Some will say that we should wait until they have repented. But that is too crude a formulation.

I am often asked, by those who know that I visit prisons, whether a particular prisoner has shown remorse. Most people who have had much contact with prisoners would feel, however, that that raises an impossible question – the question of whether some particular prisoner has repented or has shown remorse. It is no doubt of supreme significance in the sight of God. We assume that, even after the supreme sacrifice of Christ, we must repent if we are to achieve ultimate salvation. But it is impossible in most cases for those in charge to decide this, except perhaps in a family or school where the personal contact is much closer.

I will not stop to discuss the question whether there is a significant difference between remorse and repentance. Remorse is described in my dictionary as a feeling of compunction or deep regret or repentance; repentance as sorrow, regret or contrition for past action or conduct.

A supreme example of repentance and reconciliation is provided by Chuck Colson, founder of the world prison Fellowship in his memorable book *Loving God*. He was escorting a judge round the area of a prison which contained criminals condemned to death. The judge who, unknown to Colson had himself sentenced to death one of the prisoners, asked to stay behind and pray with the condemned man who had by this time been born again. The two of them joined serenely in loving testimony. That may be regarded as outside normal possibilities.

As I write these lines I have just returned from visiting a prisoner serving a life sentence for the murder of his wife, although manslaughter would have seemed a fairer verdict. With tears in his eyes he keeps repeating, "I wish that it had been me who died." I like him all the more because of his sorrow, but I beg him if only for the sake of his children to seek to build his life afresh.

The real question is: should we forgive prisoners while they are still serving their sentences and, if so, what can this forgiveness mean in practice to them?

The answer is easy enough for someone like myself who has suffered no personal injury from those who are in prison (nor have those I love). I have therefore nothing in a personal sense to forgive. I am fairly well known, I suppose, to be on friendly terms with individuals who have been involved in terrible crimes. I get many letters on this subject – some overpraise me, some are vehemently critical; some are from Christians, including the relatives of victims who feel that, while I may be idealistic enough in theory, one cannot really be expected to forgive criminals, until their offence has been purged without infidelity to the victims. In other words, without letting the victims down.

No doubt it will always be still harder to forgive injuries to loved ones than to oneself. Prof. Mackintosh, a famous Scottish theologian, in a book published some years ago called *The Christian Experience of Forgiveness*, said something here that I cannot hope to improve on. He wrote:

> The task is so very hard, not only because the injury has evoked passionate resentment, but because it looks at first sight as if forgiveness were a confession of our fault. Confession of our fault in being indignant. Whereas in our deeper mind we realise that such indignation was right and worthy, and that its absence would stamp us not as better men but worse.

Yet (Prof. Mackintosh insists, and I insist) that in spite of this fact that the forgiving of injuries done to those we love is the hardest of all moral duties, Jesus Christ has made it a condition of our being forgiven by our Father.

But what about the attitude of society and its agents? It is not, after all, the voluntary workers or the relatives of the victims who are in fact carrying out the punishment of the prisoner. In what sense can a society be expected to forgive a prisoner whom it is at the same time punishing, and probably incarcerating?

Surely (and I would like to lay tremendous emphasis on this point) we should make here the all-important distinction between our psychological attitude to the criminal and our physical treatment of him? For example, sending him to prison. Surely we should not under any circumstances fail in love, or in as much love as we can muster, towards all our fellow human beings, criminal or otherwise? Surely we should strive to purge our hearts of bitterness and hostility towards the prisoner?

Some of us, it may be, will find a vocation in offering more friendship to those who are not receiving it than to those for whom it is readily available. In other words, we will find a special vocation in helping prisoners and others under the same heading. I am thinking of all the outcasts – criminals, drug addicts and unmarried mothers, for example. An American prisoner serving a sentence of "life plus 99 years", as it was called, was helped in many ways by many people. And in his book he cried out: "What was there in me which drew from them such noble efforts?" He replied unhesitatingly: "Only the greatness of my need, but that is enough for real champions."

Christians and many others in social work among the rejected would feel that forgiveness is no more than the starting point of their labours. Once we realise the distinction between the right psychological attitude towards the convicted person and the right treatment to be accorded him, though the second will be much affected by the first, we gain, I think, a fairly clear view of how the State should behave during the period of his punishment.

It is difficult, without an appearance of irony, to talk about an abstract body like the State behaving in a spirit of love. Yet is that really so? When we talk of the State in this connection, we mean the judges, the prison officers, the welfare workers in the prisons, and all the individual men and women directly concerned with the prisoner. It is here that the Christian must do all in his power to see that the love extended is continuous. And the more repulsive the crime, the greater is the Christian challenge.

Is all this impossibly idealistic? My experience suggests the contrary. Even on the practical plane of law and order, I am convinced that kindness begets kindness and that brutality increases brutality. If we really wish to persuade convicted criminals to embark on a better way of life, we shall not do so by coercion. We shall not do so by standing aloof, or preaching to them from a pedestal of rectitude. We shall do so only by showing ourselves ready in spirit to wash their feet, as Christ once washed the feet of his disciples, forgiving them unreservedly as we ourselves must hope one day to be forgiven.

So much for criminals. Let us come nearer home. Straight away I admit that the hardest thing of all is to forgive injuries to our loved ones. Are we not entitled to feel passionate resentment? Does it not seem to be letting them down in some way, if we show goodwill to their persecutors? While there is no more difficult Christian duty than this, no one can escape it if he calls himself a Christian.

Where we ourselves have been injured, we probably do recognise in our better moments that the duty of forgiveness is clear enough. But what does this duty amount to? It may take a stoic form which is indistinguishable from indifference. The philosopher Seneca was asked why he did not hit back when somebody struck him, and replied: "If a donkey kicked you, would you kick him back?" That is the beginning of wisdom. It falls far short, however, of the Christian message which clearly enjoins not just a negative, but a positive forgiveness. Jesus Christ said:

> What man of you, having a hundred sheep, if he has lost one of them, does not leave the ninety-nine in the wilderness, and go after the one which is lost, until he finds it? And when he has found it, he lays it on his shoulders, rejoicing. And when he comes home, he calls together his friends and his neighbours, saying to them, 'Rejoice with me, for I have found my sheep which was lost.' Just so, I tell you, there will be more joy in heaven over one sinner who repents than over ninety-nine righteous persons who need no repentance (Lk 15:4–7).

We must note the positive instruction. The man does not wait for the hundredth sheep to return; he pursues it almost frantically in the wilderness, leaving the others to look after themselves.

Take now the story of the Prodigal Son. The father does

not wait for the son to arrive and throw himself at his feet. While he is still at a distance, the father runs towards him and embraces him. The lesson here is that forgiveness is the most positive, the most demanding, the most strenuous of all the virtues. The evil brought into the world by the injury done to us can only be overcome by active love.

Interlude on Suffering

The existence of widespread suffering, much of it innocent suffering, has seldom been a disturbing problem for those of strong piety. The saints have gloried in the privilege of sharing in the Passion. They have rejoiced, to use a remarkable phrase of St Paul's, in making up what is lacking in the sufferings of Christ. Ordinary people without number, possessed of Christian faith, have accepted dreadful sufferings with sublime serenity and confidence.

While I was writing this chapter, I attended an immense anti-abortion rally in Hyde Park. Many disabled persons were present, a living proof that the lives of all of us are equally valuable, and it is a great sin to destroy any life in the womb. There was, for example, a woman born without arms, who had learnt to write and drive a car with her feet. She had also stood for Parliament as an anti-abortion candidate. In the same group I was introduced to a ten-year-old boy in a wheel chair. His mother told me he was suffering from a mortal disease and had only a few months to live. Her own faith and serenity were absolute. She added that her son understood that his end was near and was perfectly resigned.

Once you have that degree of faith the mystery of suffering and the distribution of innocent suffering are left contentedly to God. But for many the question of how innocent suffering can be allowed by an all-powerful and all-loving God will always prove an impediment to the achievement of an unqualified faith. It seems necessary, therefore, to deal at some length with the intellectual issues involved.

At all times I bear in mind the distinction between the will of God in the sense of what he *permits* to happen and the will of God in the sense of what he *wishes* to happen. It would be blasphemous to say that God wished six million Jews to be murdered. But man has been given freedom and, times without number, has abused it. The problem of evil admits of a fairly simple answer. The problem of innocent suffering is very much harder. A Christian answer will, I hope, emerge below.

The problem of suffering has haunted reflective minds from the beginning of religious discussion. "The later history of religious ideas is largely the history of man's struggle with this problem" (Margaret Rose). The gods of the Greeks were numerous and amoral. In the plays of Euripides, Aeschylus and Sophocles, human suffering is central as a tragic fact – but not a problem in our sense, because the Greeks were not concerned with the difficulty of reconciling a loving God with widespread human pain. One idea, however, emerges which seems to grope after what was later to be said more clearly: the idea of the sufferer who is also a pain-bearer for others.

The Hebrews came to approach the whole problem in a fashion that led on to Christian teaching. The Crucifixion might have seemed to reduce to absurdity the belief in a world governed by a gracious providence. Yet the first Christians understood that Jesus Christ had conformed himself to the pattern of the redeeming servant who carries out to the uttermost the will of God. On Easter morning they encountered him as one who had in some way overcome sin and suffering, as well as death. Everything that has been written since by Christian thinkers confirms this message, and deepens our understanding.

Thomas à Kempis, in *The Imitation of Christ*, often referred to as the most influential spiritual book since the New Testament, preaches a doctrine of stern self-denial. But that is only the means to the end. Chapter 12 of Book Two is called: "Of the Royal Road of the Holy Cross". The note struck there is one of lyrical joyfulness. "In the cross is salvation; in the cross is life; in the cross is protection against thine enemies; in the cross is infusion of heavenly sweetness," and then, explicitly, "the cross is joy of spirit." The passage concludes: "He died for thee upon the cross, that thou shouldst bear thy cross, and for love of him be ready to die on the cross. For if thou die with him, thou shalt also live with him, and if thou art his companion in suffering, thou shalt also partake with him in glory." Thomas à Kempis goes on to explain that the cross is in fact unavoidable: "Wheresoever thou goest, thou carriest thyself with thee. Thou canst not escape thyself."

He is not concerned with the problem of suffering in the modern sense, with the problem of how a loving God could allow it. When suffering comes to us from outside, Thomas à Kempis clearly sees it as a valuable challenge. And his solution for the Christian man is simple enough. "However often or in whatever degree adversity shall befall him, he accepteth it with thankfulness and equanimity as from the hand of God and accounteth it great gain." We have already quoted his description of the way of the cross as that of daily self-denial and sacrifice; he now warns us that we are not exercised in true patience so long as we ourselves decide what, and from where, are the sufferings we submit to. "The truly patient man mindeth not by whom he is tried, whether by his own superior, or by one equal or inferior to him, whether by good and holy men, or by one that is perverse and worthless."

In other words, suffering imposed on us from outside gives us opportunities of spiritual growth superior to those which can be obtained through our own deliberate sacrifices, however heroic their purpose. As we pass from Thomas à Kempis, we are left asking: "Is he simply telling us that *any* experience can be turned, with God's help, to our spiritual advantage? Or is he arguing that pain, irrespective of motive and often springing from an evil one, brings special advantage to those who undergo it? But

Thomas à Kempis, one repeats, is not concerned to justify God's ways, but to explain to us how the spiritual man reacts to them and to persuade us to do likewise.

I will now leap across the centuries and come to two writers, men of original genius who dealt with suffering explicitly or implicitly in the nineteenth century – Kierkegaard and Dostoevsky. Kierkegaard is easily associated with suffering, but an early surprise for many will be the persistent emphasis on joy. "Each discourse," he writes in the preface to his *Gospel of Suffering*, "drinks deep enough to discover joy." In fact, the last five of the seven discourses places the word "joy" at the beginning of their chapter headings. Joy also figures largely in the first address. Not that it is by any means easy to determine what the word "joy" meant to Kierkegaard. But he makes no attempt to tackle "The question Why?", in the sense of a famous series of television programmes, presided over a few years ago by Malcolm Muggeridge. His object is practical, merciful and strengthening. "If," he says, "there is anyone who is suffering and has perhaps lost his way in many thoughts, and if he should find by these discourses a heavy moment made more light, then the author will not be sorry for the purpose that has inspired him."

We rise from the *Gospel of Suffering* as from an expert testimony. When Kierkegaard writes of suffering and its purifying effects, he carries conviction as one who knows. The joy he refers to under a dozen different headings can be traced in the last resort to a single source – our conviction that our sufferings are enabling us, as nothing else could, to find our way to Christ. The first discourse is primarily concerned with self-sacrifice, i.e. voluntary suffering, the others with suffering imposed on us against our will. But for Kierkegaard there appears to be no distinction between the ultimate benefits which, with God's help, it should be possible to derive.

There was plenty of suffering in Dostoevsky, particularly in *The Brothers Karamazov*. It is indeed an almost continuing study of suffering, but anything that could be called a doctrine of suffering must be sought in relatively few places. The essentials of the doctrine appear to be these: all of us are sinful; all of us should suffer accordingly. Until we realise this, we shall never break through the barrier of our human egotism. We shall make no spiritual progress and remain cut off from our fellow men until we are ready to face and share with all mankind the common burden of guilt. But this we can or should do fearlessly, ever mindful of the redeeming sacrifice of our Lord and assured that, in the long run, the burden of guilt will be lifted from off our shoulders.

According to Julia de Beausobie, a Russian emigrée of high spirituality (1893–1977), who spent the second half of her life in England, redemptive suffering is something peculiarly Russian which the West will never fully comprehend. No Christian is unaware that it is a fundamental element in Christian doctrine, but it means that for Russians it has always had a peculiar significance.

Moving on to the present age, we come to C. S. Lewis, whose short book *The Problem of Pain* has probably been more read than any other work on suffering in recent times. As regards evil, he makes the familiar point: "The Christian answer is that we have used our free will to become very bad and the alteration required to make us lovable by God and to realise ourselves is bound to be very painful." When he comes to suffering and, above all, to the distribution of suffering, he is less than consoling to most of us. "Some Christians", he says, "are called to a cruel martyrdom, others to nothing more than a self-submission of intention. The real problem is not why some humble, pious, believing people suffer, but why some do not!" Lewis is anxious to show that the old Christian doctrine of being made perfect through suffering is not incredible. He is readier than most of us would be to discount the natural tendency of suffering to damage the personalities of those who suffer.

In his later book *A Grief Observed*, he describes the agony he himself went through when he lost his wife.

A fine contemporary presentation of the Christian approach to suffering is contained in a small book, *Your Suffering*, by the present Bishop of Norwich, Maurice Wood. "The first stepping stone," he says, "across the river of suffering is the personal compassionate love of Jesus for those who suffer and for those who have to watch their loved ones suffer . . ."

I will quote next from a sermon given by Richard Cave, founder and chairman of the Multiple Sclerosis Society of Great Britain and Northern Ireland. He speaks as one whose wife was smitten by multiple sclerosis many years ago. Multiple sclerosis is a mysterious disease the cause of which is quite unknown, although the condition has been well recognised by the medical profession for over a hundred years. It can take a benign form, but more commonly it means inexorable progressive paralysis made more cruel by the fact that the person who suffers from it may be apparently better from time to time, only to find that the condition catches up with him again and he (or she) is worse than before. It can lead, as I say, to complete paralysis.

"I think," writes Richard Cave, "that our difficulty in coming to terms with this problem stems from the fact that we tend to look on ourselves as the focal point round which our little world revolves. What is so difficult for our human intelligence to grasp is the fact that we are all members of the mystical body of Christ. We are members of his mystical body, and we are all called on, in one form or another, to make reparation for the evil which has walked the world from the beginning of time. If we can grasp this, we can see how great is the opportunity which God gives his invalids in sharing in the suffering that is necessary for our salvation."

Richard Cave has demonstrated in his life that these are not abstract words, but are, or can be, an unwearying inspiration.

For me, the most arresting treatment of the whole problem remains that of Father Leen in *Why the Cross?* (1938). All the spiritual teaching of Christ, in his eyes, is crystallised in the statement: "Blessed are the pure in heart, for they shall see God" (Mt 5:8). He proceeds to labour two aspects of Christ's message which, at first sight, may seem contradictory, but which are complementary in his treatment. "Come to me," said Jesus, "all who labour and are heavy laden, and I will give you rest" (Mt 11:28). Jesus, it will be remembered, went on: "my yoke is easy, and my burden is light" (Mt 11:30). But he also said: "If any man would come after me, let him deny himself and take up his cross daily and follow me" (Lk 9:23).

The explanation of these two contrasting sayings is simple. "The road to happiness", says Father Leen, "is through purification of the soul. Purification involves pain, in other words suffering. This connection is not arbitrarily established by God. It arises from man's fallen nature, the element of corruption. What stands between him and God can only be eliminated by sacrifice." Father Leen points out, quoting a French theologian, that "What Christian language calls the cross, by analogy with the suffering and death of Christ, are the daily physical and moral sufferings which come from our relations with the external world and with our fallen fellow-creatures."

Suffering, therefore, whether recognised by the outside world or not, is a necessary condition of spiritual progress. But suffering in itself does not automatically create such progress. Few of us would favour the infliction of suffering on those we love in the hope that they would benefit from it. But all of us *can* benefit, and that benefit can extend to others through the redemptive power of love at a distance.

Father Leen says confidently that happiness and suffering can go hand in hand. Indeed he asserts that Christ was "constantly tried but invariably happy." It does not seem necessary to follow him in the latter statement when one remembers the agony on the cross. There is no doubt, however, that joy in suffering has been many times exhibited by the saints. For myself it remains an aspiration rather than a reality. But I have had friends, priests among them, and not a few handicapped persons, who give me an impression of what I understand it to mean.

The element of mystery cannot altogether be disposed of. It is the distribution of suffering – "Why me? Why him? Why her?" – which will always be most baffling. For me the simplest clue is the idea of solidarity of all human beings with one another, and the solidarity of all of us with a loving God, who demonstrated his ultimate solidarity with all of us by his death on the cross.

Once again, while writing this chapter I had a valuable experience. I consulted a rising moral theologian about the whole problem of suffering. He told me that the best book he had read on the subject in the last few years was Mary Craig's *Blessings*. He was not aware that I knew the book well or, incidentally, that Mary Craig had written a book about myself. The next morning I received a letter from Mary Craig beginning: "Do you realise that we have not met for a year?" A coincidence indeed! I reread *Blessings*. It is all good and moving. The last chapter is itself a small masterpiece.

Mary Craig has had two handicapped children. The first one died at the age of ten, having never recognised her. The second is a most lovable mongol. There is a striking moment in the book when, in a very dark hour, she feels that Jesus Christ is with her, and from then on she has proceeded to set a stirring example by her life and writings. Mary Craig has penetrated to the heart of the issue.

I have said before now – for example, when introducing Alf Morris's Disablement Bill to the House of Lords – that "suffering, while it often degrades, can also ennoble." But now, following Mary Craig, I would prefer to put it differently. It is not the suffering which ennobles or degrades, it is the use we make of it. No doubt the same is true under God's dispensation of any experience. But there is a special truth to be discovered and lived up to in the case of suffering.

One does not have to be a Christian to be aware that suffering can be used to elevate one's character. Nor even, though this belief is much rarer, to be convinced that one's suffering can be used to bring about the redemption of others. But the history and philosophy of the cross have provided a profoundly coherent pattern of thought and an incomparable inspiration alike for giant intellects and for a vast multitude of ordinary sufferers.

PART THREE

The Christian in Society

7   The Christian and his Social Conscience

A few words first about Roman Catholic as distinct from other Christian attitudes. My Christianity has been greatly strengthened, deepened and rendered more intellectual by my membership of the Roman Catholic Church. But the contrasts in regard to social questions between myself and other Christians have not been marked.

On abortion, there has admittedly been a difference of emphasis amounting almost to a difference of principle. When the first resolution in favour of a more liberal abortion law was put to the vote in the House of Lords in 1966, the only opponents were Catholics and one Scottish peer married to a Catholic. Lord Barrington, an Anglican peer, came up to me afterwards and asked: "Is this a Catholic thing, or can heretics take part?"

Receiving my encouragement, he set to work and initiated a mass movement of resistance. It came too late to defeat the Abortion Act of 1967 but has provided a strong resistance since that time.

Non-Catholics, of course, have played an active part in that resistance, but a particular driving force has come from Catholics. When the Abortion Bill reached the House of Lords I was Leader of the House, but left my seat to speak against it from the back benches.

Soon after the Abortion Bill became law, I visited a large abortion clinic, which the proprietors proudly told me was just "an operating hotel". I fled in disgust. But on the way out I passed through the waiting room and saw the saddest collection of young women I have ever set eyes on. My denunciations died on my lips. I asked myself, What have the Churches done for the young people who find themselves in these grim predicaments? In fact, rescue societies have laboured selflessly for many years. More recently, a good many Christians, backed by the Churches, have bestirred themselves. If it had been a Government measure, I would certainly have resigned.

I pick out this issue as one of the few cases where my Catholic principles were in sharp conflict with what was Government policy in effect, though not in name.

Apart from abortion, Catholics differ from most other Christians in their attitude to divorce and birth control. I would not feel that many Catholics have been embarrassed by this fact in their political careers. It used to be said that no Catholic could become prime minister. Then it began to be accepted that being a Catholic would be no bar to Shirley Williams becoming prime minister, Labour or SDP. Nobody now supposes that her religion would stand in the way.

Catholic education, of course, could erupt into a source of conflict but that does not seem likely at the moment. Catholics tend to feel special sympathy for Catholics in Northern Ireland. But so do many friends of justice from all denominations and none. I must, therefore, broaden our discussion to cover Christians in general. At once I must distinguish between Christian *conduct* in politics and Christian *policies*, though some overlapping is inevitable.

I hold the belief, as already indicated, that practising Christians will behave better than non-Christians on average. The converse of that is that we have special problems. If I am claiming that we are more sensitive to moral dilemmas, we have plenty in politics to be sensitive about. Politics is a harshly competitive profession. The last four prime ministers – Wilson, Heath, Callaghan and Margaret Thatcher, all good Christians, I believe – have all fought their way to the top from far down the social scale. I should be surprised to see a prime minister in this democratic age

who had been able to preserve, or develop, a deeply
spiritual life.

The accusation most often levelled against politicians is
that they say what they do not believe. I doubt if this is as
difficult a moral issue as that raised by *ambition*. I myself
resigned from the Wilson Cabinet because they were
breaking their promise to raise the school-leaving age – a
moral issue, as I saw it, but not a religious one. Three other
members of that Cabinet resigned on other matters; one of
them, George Brown, is certainly a Christian. I don't know
about the other two.

Comparing the political life with other careers, I am not
sure that the temptations are particularly great, provided
that one is a gregarious, outgoing sort of person, who can
enjoy the life. But to reach the very top, as I said just now,
requires unremitting ambition. The approach need not be
unscrupulous, but it leaves little room, indeed little time,
for spiritual development.

I come now to Christian *policies*. When I first became a
Catholic in 1940, I used to go round the country giving talks
on Catholic or Christian social principles. I have been
reluctant to do that for a long time now. The terms have
become for me too ambiguous, though I am sure excellent
talks are still being given under that heading. Since party
warfare was resumed in 1945, it has been all too obvious
that Christians and, for that matter, Catholics are totally
divided between the political parties.

One is reminded of Abraham Lincoln's second inaugural
speech, and the famous sentence: "Both prayed to the
same God, the prayers of both could not be answered."
One is forced to ask oneself whether Christian principles
have any application to the greatest social and political
problems of the time.

The central issue between the parties all these years has
concerned the distribution of wealth. As Hugh Gaitskell
used to say, "socialism is about equality," though not, of
course, absolute equality. On one occasion I introduced a

motion in the House of Lords in favour of the principle of equality, supported by my Labour colleagues; it was rejected, not surprisingly, by the Conservative ministers.

Here Christian social principles can give no more than a starting point and a criterion by which to judge the result. There are so many technical factors: the whole science of economics (if it can be called a science) comes in here. Devout Christians kneeling beside one another in prayer, as they still do in the House of Commons and the House of Lords, will rise immediately afterwards and belabour each other on behalf of their contrasted policies.

In the House of Lords there are various informal, non-party, Christian groupings. Every now and then an issue comes up that unites us automatically. We tend to be evangelical rather than Catholic, though we include all sorts, religiously speaking. We unite wholeheartedly in family matters of all kinds, in attacking abortion and pornography in all its aspects, including the proliferation of sex shops. Mary Whitehouse is not yet, alas, a member of the House of Lords, but she often comes to our discussions.

I have left till last the wide area with which I have been much associated. A somewhat satirical journalist, Alan Brien, then of the *Sunday Times*, once referred to me as "the outcast's outcast". I jumped at the title and have begged anyone who might be concerned to make sure that it is placed on my tombstone. It is, perhaps, too arrogant, almost blasphemous a claim.

Some years ago, I produced a short book on St Francis of Assisi, with immense help from Father Eric Doyle, who wrote the introduction, and others. Father Agnellus Andrew had suggested that I must have a chapter called "St Francis and the Contemporary Lepers". I shrank from that, because I would be dealing with people that I knew personally, who would not like to be referred to as lepers. I called the chapter instead "St Francis and Contemporary Outcasts", though in fact some of those concerned were not very pleased at being called outcasts. Among the groups I referred to were the mentally ill, the blacks, the homosexuals and last, but very much not least, the criminals.

Here surely we reach a specific Christian message. Jesus Christ "came to seek and to save the lost (Lk 19:10)." "I have not come to call the respectable people, but outcasts" (Mt 9:13 GNB). Or again:

> When you give a feast, invite the poor, the maimed, the lame, the blind, and you will be blessed (Lk 14:13–14).
> If a man has a hundred sheep, and one of them has gone astray, does he not leave the ninety-nine on the mountains and go in search of the one that went astray? And if he finds it, truly, I say to you, he rejoices over it more than over the ninety-nine that never went astray (Mt 18: 12–13).
> So it is not the will of my Father who is in heaven that one of these little ones should perish (Mt 18:14).

Again and again, Jesus seems to be telling us that – from the point of view of his love for them and our duty towards them – the helpless, the sick and the sinful (who have "gone astray") are on the same footing. No doubt, we have the double duty of hating the sin, and loving the sinner, though these words are not scriptural. But from the point of view of public policy, in any society known to us, it comes much more easily to perform the first task than the latter.

If we return to the categories of outcast I mentioned, the first three – the mentally ill, the blacks and the homosexuals (if they exercise self-control) – are not blameworthy; the criminals are. From one point of view, a Christian society cannot fail to discriminate between them. But from a deeper standpoint, they are all of infinite worth as the children of God; all redeemed by Christ, all capable of redemption in this world or the next; all in desperate need of our help. A society can fairly be judged by its response to their claims.

I am not likely to look down on those afflicted by mental

illness. My own breakdown in the Army would rule out that possibility. Later on (Chapter 9) I say something about mental offenders, to whom at the time of writing I am giving my top priority. They lie on the borderline between mental illness and crime. Here I am concerned with mental illness in the widest sense.

Anyone who reads and rereads the Gospels is aware that, in a high proportion of Christ's miraculous cures, devils are said to have been driven out. Christians are entitled to interpret that formulation in the light of modern psychological knowledge. For me these cures are examples of mental illness overcome by spiritual therapy. Certainly no Christian can fail to recognise a particular concern on the part of Christ for those mentally afflicted. In recent years traditional Christian wisdom and modern psychiatry have come to have much in common. "To understand all is to forgive all" – wherever those words came from they sum up effectively this new community of outlook. (I pass over the great developments recently in Christian healing through my lack of knowledge – in no way from lack of respect.)

In the world of action the impact of so much sympathy and fresh comprehension has been, up till now, distressingly feeble. It was my realisation of this which led me to initiate a debate in the House of Lords in March 1981, in which I demanded much more adequate provision for mental aftercare. At an earlier stage of my life, I had been chairman for some years of the National Society for Mentally Handicapped Children, whose needs are just as pressing and poignant as those of the mentally ill.

Following the Lords debate, on March 9th, 1981, a committee was set up under my chairmanship whose report was published in July 1983. We included in our ranks two of the leading psychiatrists in the country, three other distinguished doctors and others highly qualified. One of our most admired members was the late Lord Redcliffe-Maud, a life-long Christian champion with an unsurpassed record of public service. It was typical of him that he continued to work with us, coming up to London from Oxford, when it was obvious to him and to all of us that his days were numbered.

Our report was surely right in saying that of all the catastrophes that can afflict us none is as distressing or alienating as mental illness. One woman in five and one man in nine will require psychiatric treatment at some time in their lives. Nearly everyone, therefore, will have some experience of mental illness, either in themselves or through a near relative.

Unlike some other forms of illness, however, mental illness carries a social stigma that further disables those afflicted: it embarrasses the relatives and others who want to help. It leads to a tacit avoidance of the subject (except for disparaging jokes) by the population at large.

Our report went on to recall that about one per cent of the population are in touch with psychiatric services on any given day (over a half of them actually in-patients) and that a further one per cent will make contact during the ensuing year. This makes altogether a million people in a population of 50 million and this excludes those in need who are not receiving specialist help. The scale of the problem is indeed vast.

In a negative sense, there has been a considerable advance in public enlightenment. In the last twenty-five years the number of those confined in mental institutions has been more than halved. But this, in itself encouraging, development has not been matched by the steps to build up a positive system of community care which are presupposed by the policy of emptying the hospitals to so large an extent.

What was said above about the social stigma and the tacit avoidance of the subject of mental illness has clearly had much to do with the failure to take positive remedial action. Voluntary bodies such as the Richmond Fellowship have shown heroic initiative. But overall the community effort has up to now fallen far short of what was expected when the Mental Health Act of 1959 was passed into law.

In some social areas Christian action is inhibited by the sheer technicality of the problems involved. In the field of mental health, there will always be technical issues of subtlety and complexity. But what has been lacking hitherto has been the will to do the right thing – and there, at least, Christians should see the way forward easily enough.

So it is in race relations. Nothing that has happened in Britain in recent years can compare with the dreadful riots that swept through some of the inner cities of Britain in the summer of 1981. Lord Elystan-Morgan, speaking for the Labour Party in a House of Lords debate on October 26th, 1982, referred to the "chill of horror" that entered the heart of every responsible citizen. The riots were not race riots in the sense of battles between whites and blacks. The immediate motivation was hostility to the police; there were often pitched battles between the police and the rioters.

In earlier days my wife had been active as a member of the Africa Bureau in the cause of African emancipation. I had frequently spoken up on those lines in the House of Lords. I was somewhat ridiculed for saying that whenever I met a black man in the King's Road, Chelsea, I always said, "Good morning". That makes it sound a long time ago.

My involvement with immigrants, however, started actively about twelve years ago. I have learnt most from three West Indian friends of mine – the Rev. Ashton Gibson, Rene Webb and Greg Nowell. Ashton Gibson started the Melting Pot Foundation in Brixton, a centre for West Indians, and more recently initiated West Indian Concern in Hackney. Rene Webb and Greg Nowell, close collaborators of Ashton's from the beginning, now preside over the Melting Pot. Greg Nowell considers that the cause of the Brixton riots was a combination of high unemployment among young black people in the area and unwise police initiatives. Lord Scarman, in a notable report, does not exempt the police from blame, though he is at pains to pay tribute where tribute is possible. "The police response to the disorders once they broke out is to be commended not criticised." His report, however, was generally taken as critical of the police in many respects.

Ashton Gibson seeks to go deeper, arguing from his own Christian standpoint. He insists that it is not blatant racism but unconscious racism which is difficult to deal with, and it is very widespread.

Is it possible to discover a dispassionate assessment? Elliott Kendall, in his booklet *Christianity and Race* on behalf of the British Council of Churches, concludes:

> There is prevalent in Britain such a degree of institutionalised racism that it has created and will create the spark to set off large-scale violence in society . . . The message for us to hear as Christians is that much wrong is being done to others who are victims in a racist society. We as a nation are perpetuating racial injustice. Our greatest need is to rid ourselves of the injustices which society inflicts on black people and other minorities.

There speaks a representative Christian voice with which I am in heartfelt agreement. The practical working-out of such an attitude is confronted with endless difficulties, but at least it provides an honourable starting-point.

Homosexuality, male and female, raises issues far too complex to be pursued at any length here. But it cannot be totally ignored. As mentioned below, when the Wolfenden Report appeared in 1956, I gained a reputation as a friend of the homosexual cause which I have hardly sustained. Not very long ago an attempt was made in the House of Lords to lower the age of consent for homosexual practices from twenty-one to eighteen. After more than my usual degree of deliberation, I voted against it. Youth organisations which I much respected were alarmed by the possibilities of corruption. It appears that those who wished to lower the age to eighteen were not likely to stop there. It made me sad to disappoint some of those who had admired my earlier initiative.

As I will spell out in the next chapter, Christian principles condemn sex outside marriage whether heterosexual or homosexual. For my part, I have no doubt that a grievous wrong is done to a young person if he is introduced in adolescence to homosexual practices or confirmed in them if he is already homosexually inclined. If he does indeed become a homosexual for life he is condemned, in any state of society we can foresee, to lead a secretive existence and is denied the prospects of any normal marriage. It will be understood from what I have just said that I regard homosexuality as a painful handicap, though of course there is no possible sin in *being* a homosexual. Sublimated, it has often proved a noble inspiration. It may seem harsh that committed homosexuals should be denied by Christian principles the sexual expression of a loving relationship. There is no reason whatever why such relationships should not occur *without* sexual participation. I have known plenty of cases among men, and still more among women, where this has been a spiritual outcome.

One thing at least is certain – that any attempt to persecute homosexuals, even if they are breaking the orthodox Christian rules, is utterly opposed to Christian charity. They deserve more, rather than less, sympathy as compared with fellow citizens who do not share their handicap.

The word "outcast" may not be quite satisfactory. Those whom I have described as such do not, understandably, care for the label. Perhaps "disadvantaged" is the better word, though it loses the implication that those in question are being treated with less than Christian sympathy. Once that word is adopted, there is no limit to those who qualify. I myself, for example, was chairman for some years of the National Society for Mentally Handicapped Children. I had the privilege of carrying through the House of Lords the "Alf Morris Disablement Bill" of 1970. At the time of writing I am about to introduce a supplementary bill to help the disabled into the House of Lords.

In my book about St Francis, I mentioned, in addition to those referred to above, the unhappily pregnant and the vast army of the lonely. I devoted a special chapter to the equally vast army of the poor, at home and abroad.

"Keep close to the poor," said Father D'Arcy to me when he was preparing me for the Catholic Church. No follower of Christ will ever be very far from them in thought.

Poverty in Britain is serious enough. But neither absolutely nor relatively does it bear comparison with poverty in the Third World. It is reckoned, for example, that in South Asia alone about one half of the population is below a stringently-drawn poverty line. John Vanier's words sum it all up. What he says of Calcutta hardly exaggerates the plight of the Third World:

> The gap between riches and poverty in India is monstrous. On one side, a crowd of people, a stagnant mass, pressed together, a world of dirt; the sick, the dying – a real leprosy of humanity. And then a woman who arrives in a chauffeur-driven car, who plays golf on a huge course, who is alone with her riches. Calcutta – folly of riches and misery.

Twenty years ago, the British Labour Party, then in opposition, set itself what seemed the modest aim of devoting one per cent of the national income to helping the poorer countries. Later, there came a general agreement among the richer nations to devote 0.7 per cent to this end. But in fact our country has never contributed much more than half this percentage to this purpose, and our performance has been fairly average. We are reaching a point where it is being seriously argued that it is impossible to render help to backward countries, that we actually do more harm than good by making the effort. This reactionary doctrine is being strongly resisted by Christians. Whatever the technical difficulties, a Christian cannot fail to believe that the gross maldistribution of income between the rich and poor countries is an affront to Christian teaching.

It is easier, however, to focus our ideas on the situation in Britain which is, or should be, under our control. And here no Christian can afford to neglect a recent book such as that of Bishop Sheppard of Liverpool, *Bias to the Poor*. He has made full use of his exceptional experience in inner-city London and stricken Merseyside. His title, no doubt deliberately, is provocative. "Bias to the Poor," he writes, "sounds like a statement of political preference. My experience has been that some of the most sensible teachings of orthodox Christianity lead me to this position." He demands what he calls "a shift of power and resources".

This comes close to the perennial demand of radicals for a more equal distribution of income and wealth. Bishop Sheppard is anxious to avoid committing himself to any political party. But there can be no doubt that his diagnosis will give more satisfaction to left-wing than right-wing citizens. He recognises candidly this implication: "The call for justice," he writes, "jars on many ears. To those who broadly believe the status quo to be a just one, it seems more wounding than the demand for charity or welfare. There is an honest argument here," he goes on, "between people who truly care for the poor. To defend the status quo is not necessarily an attitude to be condemned."

Such people, says the Bishop, feel that the call for justice is somehow a personal attack on themselves or on those, whom they admire, who have gone before them. They feel as though they are being blamed, and they resent that as unfair; they feel they are prisoners of history. Nevertheless, Bishop Sheppard rejects their conclusions and, as mentioned above, demands the shift of power and resources.

Here inevitably we find ourselves returning to politics.

The Conservatives believe that their political and economic theories will, in the long run, benefit the poor. Members of the other parties, including myself, believe precisely the opposite. As a Christian one should be ultra-sensitive to the plight of the poor, and inflexibly determine to support whatever policies seem likely to improve their condition.

In what sense has God a "bias to the poor"? – to use Bishop Sheppard's phrase, which has been supported by Roman Catholic leaders. Certainly Christ says, "Blessed are the poor," and he has warned us that it will be hard indeed for a rich man to enter the kingdom of heaven. Yet unless we are committed to a life of religious asceticism we mostly are content to try to improve our standard of life and to provide our children with a better standard than we had ourselves. There will be few Christian theologians who say this is wrong. Nevertheless a man who places spiritual beyond material values is higher in the Christian scale than the man whose priorities are the opposite. What of Christ's instruction to the young man that if he wanted to be perfect he must sell all his goods and give the money to the poor? One must acknowledge this as the highest personal vocation.

8   Sex, Marriage and the Family

In 1960 the future John Paul II published a book, called *Love and Responsibility*, based on a profound study of sexual problems. He was, for many years, a professor of ethics and had obviously devoted enormous intellectual energy to sexual issues. The book was published twenty years later in England after he had become Pope: "Doctrine," he writes, "the teaching of the Church – in the sphere of sexual morality – is based upon the New Testament, the pronouncements of which on this subject are brief but also sufficient. . . ." He refers to five texts from the Gospels and two from St Paul. He begins with the pronouncement that "the moral truth most closely bound up with the world of persons is the commandment to love." From there he proceeds inexorably to proclaim the need for chastity before marriage and fidelity afterwards.

Again and again throughout the book he insists on the positive character of the Christian message. He says this in a multitude of different ways. He writes, for example:

There can be no genuine tenderness without a perfected habit of continence which has its origin in a will always ready to show loving-kindness and so overcome the temptation merely to enjoy, which is put in its way by sensuality and carnal concupiscence . . . limitation of one's freedom might seem to be something negative and unpleasant but love makes it a positive, joyful and creative thing. Freedom exists for the sake of love . . .

Some Christians have given the impression that Christians thinks of sex as bad in itself. This, of course, is nonsense. C. S. Lewis is one of many writers who have pointed out that Christianity is almost the only one of the great religions which thoroughly approves of the body. I admit that, if you come across a book called *The Joy of Sex*, you would be surprised to find that it has been written by a Christian. But there is no logical reason why it should not be. It is time that the omission was rectified.

It is known to us all that sex outside marriage, more particularly before marriage, has become much more common in recent years. There is sometimes said to be a swing away from it. Occasionally one reads a more encouraging item. On May 11th, 1983, we were told in the *Guardian*, for instance, that the Independent Broadcasting Authority had banned a public service announcement on contraception because it believed young people could be influenced into thinking that premarital sex was normal and commonplace.

It is admittedly difficult to get at the facts. In debates at the Cambridge Union in recent years, I have twice defended the Christian position of "no sex outside marriage", each time being on the losing side. But on the last occasions the most attractive champions were much more concerned with asserting their *right* to have sex when and how they chose, without interference, than with their intention of exercising that right at all freely. As always, there was strong resentment among the young women at any idea that they were promiscuous or "sleeping around". As always, there was no coherent suggestion of an alternative to the Christian tradition. There was some talk of "no sex without love", but no one seemed to find that a very helpful formulation.

I ventured the observation, in discussion afterwards, that most of the young women would be equally horrified at being told that they were virgins, or that they were not virgins. No comment was elicited.

Not long afterwards, I preached on "sex before marriage" in an Oxford college chapel and took part in discussions afterwards. Not surprisingly I came away with no hard information about the private lives of the young people. But the attitudes of what was primarily a Christian audience were reassuring.

At the Cambridge Union a young woman had won considerable approval when she told us that in her circle young men and women often spent the night together in bed without indulging in sex. Did that count as sex before marriage? I was inclined to think not.

A lady doctor who does much lecturing to senior schoolgirls has told me that she was asked repeatedly: "Will my future husband know whether I have had any sex in advance of marriage?" All therefore is not lost, but there is much ground to be recovered.

It seems to be taken for granted that this is the age of the "permissive society". I do not dispute the fact. But the phrase is capable of many definitions. We can begin with the conception of a more tolerant society, tolerant both in terms of the criminal law and public opinion. On the first plane, we have liberalised the law relating to homosexual relationships and to abortion. On the second, we show a much more lenient attitude to those who commit adultery and fornication and to those who produce illegitimate children – none of which activities was ever illegal. Divorce-law reform and the huge increase in divorces come under both our headings.

This new tolerance, this refusal to interfere by law or public opinion in the private lives of our neighbours, must be measured against the Christian doctrine that we must hate the sin, but love the sinner. In the sexual area the sin is now hated less. Not much more is done for the sinner – the prostitute, the unmarried mother. The net result is the so-called sexual revolution, a phenomenon which cannot bring joy to anyone who favours the Christian tradition, or considers seriously the effect on children.

I was sixty-five when, in 1971, I opened a debate in the House of Lords on pornography – but I had figured quite prominently before that time in debates on various aspects of the "permissive society", sometimes on the liberal, but more often on the conventional Christian side.

The Wolfenden Report of 1956 was a watershed. Not only did it propose that homosexual practices between consenting adults in private should no longer be criminal offences, it laid down the far-reaching proposition, traceable to John Stuart Mill, that no one should be prohibited by law from doing anything which did no harm to anyone else. This general philosophy was by then becoming widely accepted, but no one in the House of Commons would take the risk of raising the particular issue of homosexuality. I rushed in where they feared to tread, and initiated a debate in the House of Lords in favour of the Wolfenden proposals, though I did not press the matter to a vote. I remember a sudden qualm as I got up to speak. Was I after all on the right side? It was more than ten years before the Wolfenden proposals about homosexuality became law.

I was referred to by the present Lord Boothby as the "non-playing captain of the homosexual team". By that time I had acquired something of a reputation as a friend of homosexuals. The New Bridge for ex-prisoners, which I and others founded in 1955, was said to have been described by the Home Office as a club run by homosexuals for homosexuals. It was pointed out, I am told, that I had at that time eight children, to which the answer was given: "Oh, that's just cover."

I played no part in the passing of the Obscene Publications Act in 1959, but at the time of the *Lady Chatterley* trial of 1961 I was approached, as were many other supposed liberals, to give evidence for the defence. I replied, "I'm afraid I'm a puritan." The defence solicitor persisted: "But Lawrence was a puritan." I replied, "Not my sort of puritan."

If I was liberal on homosexuality, though always regarding the sexual act outside marriage as sinful, I followed conventional Christian lines on most other matters, and specifically the Catholic line in the case of abortion. I opposed euthanasia and artificial insemination by donor. I could not, therefore, be easily labelled a friend or an enemy of the permissive society – a phrase becoming increasingly fashionable at the time.

During my years in the Wilson Cabinet (1964–68) I concurred cheerfully in the reform of the law relating to homosexuals, and enthusiastically in the abolition of capital punishment. The introduction of a parole system and other penal reforms followed, on the whole, the lines of the report of a committee of which I was chairman. But I was one of only two members of the Cabinet who were opposed to the bill liberalising the law on abortion. It was nominally a private member's measure, but it was backed by the Home Secretary, Roy Jenkins, and other ministers. As already mentioned in the previous chapter, I took the unprecedented step of leaving my seat as Leader of the House of Lords and denouncing the bill from the back benches, with no chance of success.

Pornography is the subject for which I still appear to be best known to the man in the street. It is not so long ago that a taxi driver, dropping me at my flat, asked me, "I know you are Lord Porn, of course, but could you please tell me your other name?" Yet my connection with this unpleasant topic came about late in the day.

The libertarians had shown in 1969 the lengths to which they were prepared to go; a working party set up by the Arts Council produced a report that, in effect, argued that there ought to be no restrictions at all on what was seen and read by adults.

It was regarded by many as a signpost to the seventies. Serious alarm was expressed in March 1970 by James Callaghan, then Home Secretary. He was obviously concerned about the way things were going. He told the House of Commons that he would back up the police when they investigated complaints from the public about pornography.

Kenneth Tynan's nude revue *Oh Calcutta!* created a sensation in the summer of that year. It was described by its producer as "elegant erotica". An article in *The Times* concluded that it contributed to the general public's idea of what was acceptable. There were many protests, including one from Lord Beswick, the Labour Chief Whip in the House of Lords, and from the former Archbishop of Canterbury, Lord Fisher. I became aware, as a reader of *The Times*, that even such a leading champion of liberal legislation on obscenity as A. P. Herbert was shocked by the latest developments.

I went to see *Oh Calcutta!* and walked out halfway through in disgust. The nudity in itself did not upset me particularly. The endless dirty jokes and salacious tittering of the revue left me with an overpowering impression that corruption was in the air. It was not long since theatre censorship had been abolished, and there was a feeling of "Now we can do anything on stage, and so we must."

From the summer of 1970 to the summer of 1971 the battle for and against pornography was fairly joined. At last those opposed to pornography, including a number of prominent intellectuals, were ready to speak out and risk the resulting ridicule. Of course many of those who resisted any attempt to interfere with pornography insisted that they disliked it as much as anyone. In practice, they played into the pornographers' hands by ridiculing those – such as the heroic Mary Whitehouse and the dedicated evangelicals of the Festival of Light – who voiced the ever-wider disquiet.

Following a debate I initiated in the House of Lords in 1971, I became chairman of a committee, to investigate and counter pornography, which aroused enormous publicity and reported in September 1972. Here again, as with Mary Whitehouse and the Festival of Light, the inspiration was primarily Christian, though at least two humanists were included in our committee. In the event, we recommended a three-pronged attack on pornography. We called for the introduction of legal sanctions, *(a)* against indecent display, *(b)* against the production and sale of the more extreme forms of pornography, and *(c)* against the exploitation of the performers required.

Did our report have any effect on curbing the growth of pornography? Who can say? Things would surely have been a great deal worse if we, along with the Festival of Light and Mary Whitehouse, had not set out to stem the tide. One must admit, however, that pornography – stimulated at all times by commercial interests – is blatantly conspicuous at the time of writing. Legislation dealing with the use of children for pornographic productions and also with indecent display has been put on the Statute Book. Sex shops have greatly increased over the last ten years, but have been somewhat hampered by new legislation. Video 'nasties' are the issue of the moment.

Why do I say and why do we nearly all feel that pornography is in some sense objectionable? It is sometimes referred to, with truth, as moral pollution. In the book I wrote about St Francis of Assisi I asserted that St Francis would have treated pornography in its myriad forms as a defacement of the human body, itself the handiwork of God, and as an outrageous and defiling sacrilege. I will try to put that in modern terms. In the first place, almost everybody is disgusted by pornography of some kind. Hardly any sane person would not be revolted by a live sex show in London of the kind staged in Copenhagen. The first point to be made against pornography, therefore, is that it offends a large number of people and, in its more extreme forms, offends the large majority of people.

Next comes the question of lasting moral damage. One admits the extreme difficulty of demonstrating that any particular piece of pornography is likely to cause damage, but few suppose that anyone who spent a large amount of his time revelling in pornographic productions would be morally unaffected. A diet of filth will, beyond all question, corrupt a nation. Finally there is the degradation of the performers, including children, who are involved in the production of a pornographic work. Their exploitation illustrates the depths to which the pornographic industry drags down all those concerned alike with it, producers or consumers.

When one turns to actual changes of conduct over the post-war period one is on much more hazardous ground. In Chapter 9 I deal with the immense increase of crime for which figures, however imperfect, can be readily produced. In the moral sphere we cannot ignore the enormous increase in the number of divorces. To quote Robert Chester, a sociologist from the University of Hull: "British marriages today are divorcing at the rate of one in three. In America it is nearer one in two . . . We have been changing very fast . . . up to half a dozen years ago the figure was more like one in ten."

On the subject of divorce, Mary Kenny, a former champion of libertarianism but now an invaluable supporter of fidelity and chastity in family life, points out that in the sixties it was thought, and predicted by a Lord Chancellor, that divorce would eventually settle down at around 40,000 to 50,000 petitions a year. In 1973 there were in fact 106,000 divorces in England and Wales. It was still thought that the figures, and the people whose lives they represented, would settle down, but in 1980 the figure was 170,000. There is no sign whatever that the figures will settle down. This is the other, and horrifying, side of the liberation applauded by sociological commentators.

We must admit that fidelity to marriage vows and commitment to a lifelong partnership has been much impaired. David Thompson, in his account of England in the twentieth century, says unequivocally: "The most important cultural and intellectual phenomenon of the years after 1945 was the upheaval and extent of abandonment of traditional values and the quest for new values felt to be more appropriate to life in a rapidly changing materialistic and scientific civilisation."

He goes on to say that sexual ethics underwent a rapid and drastic change, just as views on what constituted public decency changed markedly where literature, the stage and television were concerned. The Obscene Publications Act of 1959, the court's decision to allow the unexpurgated version of *Lady Chatterley's Lover* to appear, and the Wolfenden Report on homosexuality are regarded by him as key events.

These new, allegedly more humane, more civilised and more libertarian attitudes are, of course, in total conflict with traditional Christian values; in my eyes they represent a tragic decline in human morals.

Mrs. Thatcher delivered a resounding speech on July 26th, 1982, to the Institute of Electrical Engineers. Her subject was "Women in a Changing World". But what she had to say about the family is highly relevant here. She said:

> Throughout history great emphasis has been laid on the importance of the family, but in family matters today there are some very disquieting features. For example, in 1882 there were 43,000 illegitimate births in England and Wales. Some eighty years later, in 1960, there were approximately the same number. In 1980 the numbers had risen to 77,000. Worse still the number of girls who conceived children under the age of sixteen has risen from 6,600 in 1970 to 8,100 in 1979. Further, the number of juvenile offenders has doubled in less than twenty years rising from 100,000 in 1965 to nearly 200,000 in 1977. Moreover, today one in ten marriages is expected to break down after five years and one in three after thirty years.

All this badly needed saying from the top level. She did not deal with abortion in her talk, but between 1969 and 1979 the total number of legal abortions rose from fifty per 1,000 to 119 per 1,000, a percentage increase of 138.

A book I heartily approve is *Sex in the Real World*, a

Lion paperback by Lewis Smedes, professor of theology and the philosophy of religion at Fuller Theological Seminary, USA. "The most obvious fact," says Professor Smedes, "about today's single people with respect to sex is that they have grown up in a sexually superstarred era. They have been bombarded by sexual stimuli as no other generation has." Certainly, films, the media, erotic writing of all kinds, ruthless advertising, have exercised a tremendous pressure. At least as potent an influence have been technological innovations which have greatly weakened the traditional fears which seem to support morality. To quote Prof. Smedes again: "Conception, infection and detection have been – it is supposed – done in respectively by the Pill, the antibiotic and the back of the car."

Personally I would be inclined to lay just as much emphasis on a new climate of free discussion which extends far outside the sexual area. Today, far more than hitherto, it is not possible to carry conviction simply by referring to long-established values, whether religious or otherwise. Everything has to be justified by some kind of argument whether sensible or otherwise. Again, speaking personally, I cannot regret the much freer discussion which, for example, has distinguished the Churches in recent times. But as a result Christian values are endangered unless those who hold them dear become much more active than hitherto in thinking out and defending their position. I have moved from the religious to the secular. As always, they overlap. It is impossible to discuss sex outside marriage without referring to marriage itself.

Can we not concede that a lifelong marriage partnership is the ideal? Surely we can go on to agree that adultery is a threat to it? Not, of course, the only threat or always fatal to marriage. Violence and drink and persistent bad temper are strong rivals for the dishonour; but adultery must be seen as a source of widespread damage and destruction of marriage.

But that, I hope, being accepted, where does sex before marriage come in? I am submitting that fornication, i.e. sex before marriage, leads naturally to adultery, i.e. sex after marriage, and so plays a deadly part in ultimately undermining marriage.

Of course I am not suggesting that this is an invariable sequence. We all know, I am sure, of many cases where this gloomy result does not follow. But I am talking about an ineluctable trend. I refuse to regard it as a coincidence that the great expansion of sex before marriage has gone hand in hand with the enormous increase in divorce and with the equally staggering increase in illegitimate births. No one looking at these trends can fail to see a coherent pattern, a dominant atmosphere of which sex before marriage is at once a cause and effect. The traditional teaching of the Church about the perils inherent in sexual licence has been tragically confirmed by evidence which lies all around us. In spite of the intellectual distinction of some of those I have mentioned earlier, it would be ludicrous to attempt to discover a basis there for happy marriage.

It should not be necessary for me to retell the story of the woman taken in adultery. Christ said to her: "Neither do I condemn you; go, and do not sin again" (Jn 8:11). Whether the sin under discussion is sexual or otherwise (and most sins, after all, are non-sexual), we must never fail to hate the sin but love the sinner. It is not easy for most of us to do both at the same time. Christian compassion imposes on us a never-ending obligation to follow Christ when he said: "I have come not to call respectable people, but outcasts" (Mt 9:13 GNB).

For many years now I have been involved with men and women in prison, some of them convicted of horrifying crimes. I am not likely to say or feel that sex before marriage is the last word in sinfulness. But nothing will alter my conviction that it is *wrong*, not just because the Churches say so, but because it plays a major part in damaging morally those who take part in it and in the end the whole of society. Whether one is or is not a believing Christian, one should be able to see in sex outside marriage a type of action contrary to the laws of our human nature.

But the Christian ideal will never prevail unless its exponents are able to render its ultimate vision more attractive than any other. Unless they can communicate their conviction that in Christian marriage one learns what it really means to love.

9   Crime and Punishment

Christians permeated with the doctrine of forgiveness believe that they have a special contribution to offer to the whole problem of crime and punishment. But the events of recent years have interfered cruelly. When I became a prison visitor in Oxford just before the Second World War, there were, in the country as a whole, 10,000 people in prison. When I opened the first House of Lords debate on prisons in 1955 there were 20,000, and now there are over 44,000, of whom 1,400 are women, with further increases expected.

By and large, the increase in crime in Britain and the increase in the prison population have gone forward in step. The Chief Constable of Manchester, John Alderton, pointed out in 1982 that in the thirties there were 500,000 indictable offences committed per year in Britain. In 1981 the figure was three million. Figures such as these in Britain and other comparable countries have inevitably damaged the quality of penal discussion.

The reasons given for the appalling increase of crime are as variegated and unsubstantiated as they were when I undertook an inquiry into the causes of crime for the Nuffield Foundation in the mid-1950s. The broken home, more common than ever today, and the upbringing in a criminal "sub-culture" are important factors though no more quantifiable than they were. Penalties have been growing in severity rather than diminishing. There is no validity in the claim that lighter sentences are blameworthy.

When I was carrying out the Nuffield inquiry, poverty was alleged to be a primary factor, but that view could not be supported by the evidence. Since then there has been a great improvement in the standard of living, in spite of a relative stagnation in Britain and abroad in the last few years. We are now sometimes told that this new affluence is the blameworthy factor. But this explanation is as undocumented and unconvincing as the other.

The increase in crime is so widespread in Western industrial countries that one is tempted to continue to search for general causes. I have little doubt myself that it must be connected with a diminished regard for authority, whose existence cannot be disputed, and which has a good side as well as a bad. There is far less "touching of caps", literally and metaphorically, and who can regret this development? In the Catholic Church, for instance, since Vatican II, there has been much more openness of discussion, much less readiness to take everything on trust from the nearest religious authority. This may have made life harder for the priesthood, but it has provided a wonderful renewal for the Church as a whole. I cannot see these, or similar steps in the secular sphere, being reversed. They are an inevitable outcome of the democratic age, but we are paying a heavy price for them in the form of a diminished respect for law and order.

Can the increase in crime be attributed in a still wider sense to a general decline in morality? Until recently I have been reluctant to accept this broad conclusion, but it is, I fear, irresistible – though, of course, the decline is in no way irreversible. I have often said, and still believe, that we are a more humane society than in pre-war days. The Welfare State I still applaud wholeheartedly, but I ruefully reflect that it was already established thirty years ago. At the time of writing it seems possible that we shall witness the return of certain Victorian virtues, but increased compassion does not seem likely to be numbered among them.

Since I first became involved with prisoners over forty

years ago, the philosophy of punishment has never ceased to occupy my thoughts. In 1961 I published a small book on the subject following fairly traditional lines, while maintaining a Christian emphasis. I distinguished four main elements in a just sentence: not only deterrence, reform, what would now be called "containment", but also what I still call "retribution". I recognised then, and it would be still truer today, that that word carries such vengeful undertones that it might be discarded in favour of something more acceptable. It is, in any case, a word full of ambiguity. In the Lords' debate on capital punishment in 1957 my use of the term provoked both the Archbishop of Canterbury and the Archbishop of York to rise simultaneously in an attempt to clarify the concept. In my book I pleaded, as I still plead, that in any just punishment the severity of the penalty should be appropriate to the magnitude of the crime. Maybe "fairness" would be a better word than retribution.

I also called for the introduction of a larger element of reparation. Such reparation would, ideally, be made by the criminal to the victim. But obviously in many cases the criminal would not be in a position to make atonement, even where atonement was theoretically possible. I demanded, therefore, a comprehensive scheme of reparation from the State. Some years later a beginning was made along these lines.

What I did not anticipate twenty years ago, when the crime rate was still relatively low, was the intense public hostility to criminals that could be generated, with the help of the popular press, by the continuous increase in crime. Nowadays one is often confronted with the argument that public opinion would not stand this or that act of justice or mercy. I have protested, on occasion, that to allow such alleged public feeling to prevail reduces us to the level of the mob rule or lynch law of the southern states of America in their worst days. But such protests have been usually brushed aside.

Myra Hindley, convicted with Ian Brady for her share in the horrendous Moors murders – though I shall always think that her part was minimal – provides one example among many. She has been in prison for nineteen years. She has not yet been even considered for parole, i.e. allowed to come before a local Parole Board. Yet no one who knows her believes that she would be any danger to the public if she were released on parole. It is over twelve years since she was in Category A (the classification reserved for dangerous prisoners). A former chairman of the Parole Board admitted to me verbally and in writing that she is not in any way dangerous. She has taken an Open University degree. She has received much help from the priests of her communion. One of them told me that if and when she is released he would be happy to find accommodation for her in his house. Her brother-in-law has said the same.

If any rules of natural justice were being followed she would long ago have been released on parole. Political timidity is the sole reason for her continued incarceration. People sometimes say to me, referring to Home Office ministers, "Do you think they will ever dare let her out?" I refuse to believe that they never will. But the very fact that the question should be asked implies that public opinion will always be violently opposed to her parole. But what is this public opinion, and how does it come to be formed? The popular newspapers, apart from the *Daily Mirror*, have a sorry record here. Some years ago the *News of the World* published a supremely vicious attack. Within an hour, Myra Hindley had been violently assaulted by a disturbed young woman in Holloway to the point where she required plastic surgery.

In the autumn of 1983, the *Sun* newspaper published articles about her, prominently featured and advertised, for five consecutive days. They ran into trouble with the law when they began printing long extracts from the submission she made five years earlier to the Parole Board. But they were able to inculcate a good deal of hatred and, at the end of the five days, they announced that they had had hundreds of letters applauding their stance. Immediately afterwards Myra Hindley told me that she herself had had hundreds of letters sympathising with her. There wasn't room for all of them in her cell.

I will return below to the general question of the connection between public opinion and penal policy. I will make one comment here. Christians have individually responded – no one more so than Cardinal Hume – to the instruction: "I was in prison and you came to me" (Mt 25:36). But in the formation of public opinion their collective voice has been sadly muted.

Penal reformers are asked repeatedly, "Why don't you do something for the victims?" In fact, most of us have been concerned with the welfare of victims for many years. In the last twenty years there have been only five debates on victims in the House of Lords – four initiated by myself. In 1978 I led an inquiry into the whole subject and in 1979 introduced a private member's bill based on the findings of the resulting committee.

A little more, only a very little more, is being done for victims than it was. The voluntary bodies are at last beginning to grow rapidly and deserve much commendation, but the scale of operations is still small. When I am told, "You can't be on the side both of the victim and the criminal," I reply, "Of course I can, every Christian must be. Victims and criminals alike are human beings. Christ would be concerned with both." Laudable attempts are made from time to time to bring victims and criminals together. They tend to be reluctant to meet.

In this connection I will turn to the story of Shane O'Doherty, who is serving life. He is a young idealist from a much respected home in Derry. One of eight children, he was still at school, intending to follow his brothers and sisters to college, when the tragic events of "Bloody Sunday" occurred in Derry. He dashed off to join the IRA immediately, as did a number of his contemporaries. But he went further than most of the others. He obtained a position in charge of bombs, and distributed letter bombs to various people in Northern Ireland and England. When still only eighteen he was arrested and brought to England. He is serving his life sentence here, in spite of having no connection whatever with this country, apart from distributing the bombs. It was never part of his intention to take life, but a number of his victims were badly injured – two of them lost a hand.

After a long period of meditation in solitary confinement, he totally renounced the IRA. His views were widely disseminated at his request. He has come to adopt a position of complete Christian pacifism. His mother believes that, when eventually he is released, he will seek to become a missionary priest in the Third World. He has revealed a passionate desire to make atonement for the suffering he has inflicted – something that is almost unknown in my experience. As a first step, he has obtained, with difficulty, permission from the Home Office for his victims to be approached and asked whether they would accept his profound apologies. Of those who could be reached, about half were willing, half unwilling.

Both Cardinal Hume and the Bishop of Derry (for whom he was once an altar boy) have shown a special interest in Shane. I think they would agree with my description of him as the "true penitent", to borrow a phrase from Robert Louis Stevenson's *Ebb Tide*. The harsh realities of long-term imprisonment have not been mitigated by his repentance. One can only hope that his profound remorse will not be blurred, as too often in the case of prisoners, by bitterness against his treatment.

Can imprisonment ever be justified by Christian standards? Some years ago I listened to an address by a prison governor which began, "Yes, I am a prison governor. I know you don't think much of prisons. You may prefer mutilation, or transportation, or execution, or you may have other ideas which have also been tried and been rejected. But in the end, for serious crimes, you may find yourself driven back to prison as the least evil of the methods required to preserve a civilised society from total disruption . . ."

That is roughly my own point of view, or part of it. To incarcerate human beings in prison is to deny them the freedom which is usually judged essential for moral growth. It is to produce relationships between the prison staff and their charges which are, at the best, a form of benevolent slavery. It is to deprive criminals of family life and normal sexual outlets. It is to herd offenders together in a fashion well calculated to turn them into hardened criminals, graduating in a "university of crime". It should be resorted to only where there is no other conceivable option.

In recent years a number of alternative remedies, alternative punishments, have been worked out on paper, and to a limited extent put into operation. Some of them involve little more than subjecting delinquents to inconvenience – for example attendance at a centre on Saturdays. Others, such as community service orders, bring into play the constructive idea of working under supervision for the community. Penal reformers of all kinds, and many others, have demanded the strengthening of such alternative remedies. But the Home Office, under various ministers and governments, who must accept the responsibility, are still convinced that more prisons must be built. They still show little conception of the part that might be played by the alternative remedies.

The economic arguments strongly favour treatment or punishment *outside* institutions. It is vastly cheaper. The authorities usually reply by pointing to the need for increased supervisors in the short run. But the long-term gains would be so great that this argument is treated by many of us as highly disingenuous. The real reason, I conclude, is a feeling that the public would be horrified if thousands of prisoners were released. They would be frightened, even if most of the offenders had committed only minor crimes. There is still enough of a punitive instinct to produce a widespread feeling that prisoners were escaping their just punishment.

Here is one more illustration of the challenge to the Christian conscience. Some improvements have admittedly been introduced in recent years. Of these the most notable have been the institution of parole, first recommended by a committee of which I was chairman in 1964. But the huge increase in the prison population has more than cancelled out the reforms. The reluctance to rely on alternative methods of punishment becomes more shocking every year. Overcrowding in 1983 was worse than ever. Prison governors have joined penal reformers in denouncing it. The then Mr. Whitelaw, Home Secretary from 1979 to 1983, called on the judges to pass shorter sentences. It is now accepted, after many official and unofficial inquiries, that the sentences passed in England are abnormally high. They are twice as high in England as they are in Scotland. One thing at least we can be sure of: without a more enlightened sentencing policy there will not be much penal progress.

What is striking in Britain and elsewhere is the growing gulf between what might be called "enlightened" and "mass" opinion, with the judges still reluctant to pass sentences out of line with what they imagine to be public feeling. In the last twenty years there has been a great expansion in criminological studies in Britain, which previously barely existed here. Under their influence and that of psychiatry there is much more understanding of the mind of the individual criminal. Though suffering the limitations of being secular and non-judgmental, the new thinking has fitted in well in practice with the Christian tradition of forgiveness.

In the laudable emphasis on overcrowding, the long-term prisoners, who for the most part are not overcrowded, are neglected. Even penal reformers hesitate to dwell on their sufferings. The physical conditions under which long-term prisoners live are less physically degrading than those in the local prisons, but the total spiritual degradation involved is still more incontestable. Life prisoners, in particular, can be held in a state of near despair, being given for many years no indication when, if at all, they could hope to emerge from prison.

The Criminal Justice Bill of 1982, as I and others pointed out repeatedly at the time, does nothing whatever for long-term prisoners. I have, on various occasions, pleaded that prisoners who have served ten years should automatically be considered for parole. In 1983, in the debates in the House of Lords, the proposition was supported by the Labour Party, the Liberals, the SDP and certain eminent independents. Lord Hunt, the first chairman of the Parole Board, spoke strongly in favour of it. It was defeated by the Conservative Government and their faithful supporters.

Life prisoners, and other long-term prisoners, are not a category that arouse much sympathy. They may well have been convicted of dreadful crimes. Even Christian reformers find difficulty in remembering that when Christ said, "I was in prison and you came to me" (Mt 25:36), he did not mean that he was necessarily innocent or convicted of a petty offence. But as I have said in the House of Lords, "These prisoners have something in common with all of us in this House. They are members of the human race." Christ died for them as much as for us, the "goodies". The struggle for more humane attitudes towards long-term prisoners will continue during my lifetime and in the years beyond. So, I am afraid, will the instinctive urge to sweep the whole subject under the carpet.

There is general agreement today, among both those who wish prisoners well and those who do not, that prison does not usually reform prisoners, that it is likely to do them more harm than good, and that the longer the sentence the greater the likely harm. The idea, moreover, that longer sentences are more likely to deter potential criminals than short ones is also discredited by Home Office research. This latter conclusion would not seem to have percolated through to the man in the street. A general cynicism about prison treatment is increasingly widespread.

Inside the prisons I would say that the average governor or assistant governor is more enlightened today than yesterday. The number of social workers inside the system has much increased since I first became involved. There are many prison officers who would gladly undertake social responsibility. When I opened the first debate on prisons in the House of Lords in 1955, my main constructive point was that prison officers should become social servants rather than turnkeys, but in a quarter of a century little progress has been made in that direction. Bewilderment about their function is a fair description of the prison service today. Most of them are average human beings, and not a few spiritually motivated. At present, like the prisoners, they look up and are not fed.

I return to a fundamental question touched on earlier. How far should public opinion affect penal policy? The recent history of the argument about capital punishment should be helpful here. At the same time I will discuss that issue from a Christian angle.

Soon after the general election of 1983, a strong move was made in the House of Commons to restore capital punishment. Some of the omens seemed propitious. The Prime Minister was known to favour restoration. A number of Tories elected for the first time were understood to share that opinion. On the other hand, as the debate drew near, it was reported that the Secretary of State for Northern Ireland, the Lord Chancellor (speaking it would seem for the judges generally), the Lord Chief Justice, and the former Chief Commissioner for the Metropolitan Police were among those coming out against hanging.

In the event, the proposal to reintroduce hanging was comfortably defeated. The arguments on both sides were thoroughly familiar to those of us who have been involved in this controversy for many years, though the terrorist situation in Northern Ireland gave a special twist to the discussion.

A few days before the debate I took part in a long radio debate with Mr. Raymond Johnston, director for many years of the Festival of Light and, in its new manifestation, *Care*. He is a staunch Christian friend with whom I have collaborated on a number of Christian issues, including pornography, abortion and the threat to the Christian family. I was frankly amazed to find him ready and eager to state the case for hanging, though I had become aware that some eminent evangelicals were leaning that way. The leaders of the Churches, Catholic and Protestant, had come out against capital punishment with more than usual clarity.

The hope was expressed before the radio programme that we would not involve ourselves in statistics, but would stick to "the moral issues". I could promise the first, but not the second.

In the preliminary talks, and in the programme itself, I insisted that here, as in other social connections, it is impossible to conceive of a purely moral discussion that paid no attention to the consequences of the projected policy. In the case of hanging, the question of whether capital punishment is or is not a unique deterrent is a prime consideration, though not the only one.

I pointed out that in 1930 only William Temple, later Archbishop of Canterbury, was prepared to give evidence against capital punishment to the select committee. By 1957 the voting among the bishops in the House of Lords was ten to one against. In 1983, the Synod voted crushingly against it.

What had brought about this remarkable transformation in official Christian attitudes after nineteen and a half centuries of Christian thinking? There is no doubt whatever about the answer. Thirty years of intense research throughout the world had demolished the gut reaction that capital punishment was a unique deterrent. The one strong argument for capital punishment is that by taking one *guilty* life, one saves one or more *innocent* lives. No serious person who looks into the facts can believe that any longer.

Raymond Johnston did not rest his main argument on the deterrent effect and therefore could not be swayed by any demonstration that hanging was not a unique deterrent. He found what was, for him, a much more fundamental argument for supporting it.

For him, both revelation and reason could be summed up in the pronouncement in Leviticus that "He who kills a man shall be put to death" (24:17). Nothing would shake him in his conviction that capital punishment for deliberate murder is sanctioned by divine law and also by deep natural instinct.

I found, and find, the reference to the Old Testament extremely unconvincing. Two points at least occur to me immediately. One, the first recorded murderer is Cain, but he was not put to death. He was set loose as a vagabond on the earth. Two, if the Old Testament were taken literally, the list of capital offences would shock even the hardest of present-day hardliners. I mentioned earlier those who cursed their father or mother. Among many other groups, those who committed adultery would be executed. It seems impossible to accept the Old Testament as a guide to contemporary ethics. Admittedly Christ said: "I have come not to abolish [the law and the prophets]; but to fulfil them" (Mt 5:17). But in fact, in the Sermon on the Mount (Mt 5), he transformed it. "An eye for an eye" becomes "Love your enemies".

What, however, of the argument that there is a natural justice in capital punishment for murder? In my *Idea of Punishment* I accepted retribution as having a place in punishment. But in a just punishment it can only be one element, combined with deterrence, prevention, reform and reparation. If you execute someone, you exclude automatically every possibility of reformation or redemption in this life. For that reason, though not for that reason alone, it must conflict with any Christian idea of punishment.

One hardly needs to mention the practical objections, the brutalising atmosphere, the uncertainty of guilt and innocence, the likelihood of a large mental factor, the impossibility of assessing it . . . The Christian who is prepared to put aside prejudice, study the evidence and spend time on his knees, should be able to find only one answer.

Was public opinion defied by Parliament when they rejected hanging? And, if so, in what sense? Public opinion on this matter has never been explicitly articulated. Public opinion polls have no binding authority. If there were ever a referendum on hanging, as there was on British entry into Europe, the abolitionists would launch a campaign as well-informed as it was passionate. For the first time the general public would be educated on the evidence against capital punishment. Who can say what the result would be? Certainly the overwhelming support for hanging would be much whittled down.

Do I seem to be proving too much? Am I raising doubts about my democratic convictions? If so, I must clarify my argument. The public have strong emotions about penal policy but very little information. Penal reformers are a tiny minority. We have long been aware that there are no votes in penal reform. More recently the marketing consultants are probably informing the central offices that penal reform is a vote loser. Of course, one would like to see that situation altered, but while it lasts it is gratifying to find, as in the recent hanging decision of the House of Commons, that members are prepared to place their informed consciences above the findings of the opinion polls and the pressures of their constituents.

At the time of writing, the present Home Secretary, Mr. Brittan, has proclaimed an altogether tougher attitude to serious offenders, especially those convicted of crimes of violence. Much controversy has been aroused, in which I am expecting to participate in the direction adverse to Mr. Brittan. On December 14th, 1983, I introduced into the House of Lords yet another motion on parole, expressing grave disquiet about the new trend of penal policy.

There is a large category of prisoners who can be described as mentally afflicted, slightly or seriously. Few concerned with prison administration would deny that in an ideal system many prisoners would not be in prison, but in some form of hospital. It is rash to generalise, but they probably comprise ten per cent of the prison population.

One personal story must suffice as an illustration, that of someone whose life has been spent in and out of prisons and mental homes, a person obviously not typical of the criminal world as a whole, though typical of a fair section of it. Roy was educated in State schools and left grammar school at seventeen with good "O" levels and three "A" levels. Why did he not go to university? Because, he told me, "even at that time I had a penchant for the physical things in life, clothes and cars – money, I mean." One year after leaving school he was in trouble with the law for stealing cars, and stealing from cars. Having been injured in a car accident, he decided: "Not having one of my own, I will take other people's." And during the subsequent twenty years, with intervals in prisons and mental hospitals, he has pursued that policy. If I ask him why, after having had lunch with me at the House of Lords, he goes straight off and breaks into someone's car, he replies candidly: "If I knew the answer to that I would not do it."

He has great ability and has successfully challenged the Home Office on points affecting censorship. He has been flown to the European Commission of Human Rights at Strasbourg to state his case, which he won. No one can possibly regard him as devoid of moral principle or good feeling, as I know when he has helped me in a voluntary capacity. Yet, at times, he acts in a manner so antisocial that society must be protected against him. It seems to be a requirement of a civilised society that we should make the general assumption that men and women are responsible for their actions, and that, if they infringe the law seriously, they must be punished.

But society has up to now shrunk from facing the moral and practical problems which are presented by offenders whom we label "abnormal" or "mental". Not surprisingly, the provision for them has so far been totally inadequate. At the time of writing, my friend, Peter Thompson, who is dedicated to this as to other neglected causes, and I myself have tried to initiate an inquiry with much expert help into the whole question of mental offenders. Psychiatrists, judges, social workers of all kinds, must each make a large contribution if mental offenders are to be dealt with adequately for the first time. The Christian role is paramount.

10   Peace and War

Is there a distinctive Christian attitude to war? Most Christians would like to think so. I think so myself. But at first sight it seems hard to substantiate the claim. Starting from Christian premises, I have arrived at my own conclusions. I cannot pretend that they are binding on all Christians. The argument between pacifists and non-pacifists persists within the Churches as it does outside them.

In the great debate in the Church of England Synod in February 1983, the Archbishop of Canterbury began his speech by declaring: "In the course of this debate on nuclear weapons and Christian conscience a large measure of ground common to all Christians has already been mapped out." But a dispassionate observer might be forced to conclude that the differences were as pronounced as the similarities.

The Bishop of Salisbury's working party had produced the report which gave rise to the debate in the Synod which, in the event, rejected the report. It contains a chapter entitled "Theological and Ethical Considerations". It cannot be said that these considerations had much effect on the central argument. The report quotes one particular statement which has been endorsed by Lambeth conferences for half a century – that war, as a method of settling international disputes, was incompatible with the teaching of our Lord, Jesus Christ. The working party described this announcement as "unquestionably consonant with the Christian faith". "It admirably expresses," they say, "what many Christians actually feel about war." But they admit that it offers no practical guidance in trying to decide whether a specific war is legitimate. "In particular it does not enable us to pronounce on the legitimacy of nuclear war." They assert that what is required is something "more specific". "Something which takes all the relevant information into account, which dares to make technical judgments and shuns the immunity afforded by more general statements." The report then attempts – with a wealth of expert, if controversial, argumentation – to produce a large slice of policy for a British government in the field of foreign affairs and defence.

Canon Oestreicher, a member of the Salisbury committee, spoke powerfully in favour of its proposals. The report, he said, "simply recognises that a small and relatively weak nation like our own can actually do something to break the log-jam. It would not be just a little gesture; it would be recognised as something very significant." His words no doubt reflected the opinions of the minority of the Synod who supported the working party.

The Archbishop of Canterbury explained his reasons for reaching conclusions in precisely the opposite sense. How do Christians, he asked, fulfil their vocation and prime moral duty to be peacemakers in a world which has rejected the order given to it by its Creator? The Archbishop said:

> I regret to say that I do not find the recommendations contained in *The Church and the Bomb* and further amplified in the Bishop of Salisbury's amendment to be entirely coherent or convincing. I do not believe that unilateral measures of the kind suggested will in fact have the effect of getting multilateral reductions moving.

He went on to say that the policy recommended by the working party would have the effect of making agreed disarmament not more likely but *much less* likely (my italics).

In passing, one must quote one or two sentences from the Bishop of Birmingham in the same debate. "We need to remind ourselves," he said, "that there are no direct answers from the New Testament because we find there only the ethics of personal action. We are concerned today not with personal behaviour but with the morality of the State, and Jesus gave us no teaching on that!" Personally I would feel that that was going altogether too far, but the statement was not challenged. It is a simple fact that sharply different views about war in general, and about any particular war, have always been held within Christianity, though the so-called "just war" theory occupied a central position for hundreds of years.

When I spoke at a famous public school I was asked by a boy (I believe that he was the CND secretary), "Are Christians prepared to use force in any circumstances?" Which leads to the related question, "Can one be a sincere Christian without being a pacifist?" Personally I think so. Throughout the centuries most Christians have thought so. But long before the coming of nuclear weapons, many Christians have thought not.

This issue was cloaked for many of us for a long time between the wars. The League of Nations had emerged from the 1914–18 war as the one apparent guarantee that "It would never happen again." It was reasonable to believe in the principle of collective security, to calculate that no country would indulge in aggression if it knew that the whole world would be ranged against it. It was not till Mussolini invaded Abyssinia in 1935 that the principle was put to the test. Then (as we used to say, and as I still say) it was not the League of Nations that failed the world, it was the great powers who failed the League.

The issue of collective security, involving force in the last resort, versus pacifism was posed dramatically at the Labour Party Conference of 1935. I shall never forget the emotional appeal of George Lansbury, the leader of the Party, a dedicated pacifist. "Those," he cried, "as Christ told us in the Garden, those who take the sword will perish by the sword." But the voice of Ernest Bevin, speaking with equal passion on behalf of collective security, prevailed. Lansbury resigned. Collective security became the established policy of the Labour Party. The Conservatives had recently announced their adherence to it, but there were already indications that their attachment to it did not go deep.

The principle of collective security was not honoured and world war drew closer and closer. The Nazi bid for conquest, with all its attendant brutalities, presented Christians with the stark choice of fighting Hitler or allowing him to subjugate the world. The great majority of Christians chose the way of armed resistance. But there were not a few who kept the pacifist flag indomitably flying. By the end of the war, the Nazi tyranny had been broken but another far-reaching threat to world peace had been established in Soviet Russia. From that day to this the tension between East and West has continued.

Hopes were cherished between the wars that a world organisation and the operation of the principle of collective security would guarantee peace. They have never come close to being realised. The constructive part played by the United Nations in countless ways must on no account be minimised. But the United Nations has been able to contribute little, if anything, to mitigating the East/West confrontation.

The defence policy and much of the foreign policy of the West has, since the war, been primarily based on the Atlantic Alliance. That Alliance would be meaningless and even sinister if it had not been, from the beginning, an ineluctable response to the aggression of Soviet Russia. It would be incredible on any assumption other than that of the Soviet menace that Britain, for example, would be spending £17,000 million a year on armaments.

I was Minister for Germany from 1947 to 1948, and sat beside Ernest Bevin at the Council of Foreign Ministers in

December 1947. When I had become Minister in the spring, he asked me to meet him in Berlin on his way back from the Moscow Conference. He told me then that he remained confident, though others were not, that a settlement with the Soviet Union would be reached at the December meeting. For three weeks he strove desperately to prevent the world falling apart into two hostile halves.

There came a day when General Marshall, the American Secretary of State, said bluntly that in his opinion it was no good going on. Bevin did not often consult me at the table, but this time he asked me quietly what I thought. Personally, I felt sure that this was the end, but knew that, next day and for long afterwards, he would bitterly regret it if he did not labour for reconciliation until the clock struck twelve and beyond. I suggested that he should ask for a postponement, and that is what I think he would have done, but before his turn came Bidaut, the French Foreign Secretary, strongly supported Marshall – so Bevin could only concur.

Next morning, as I had expected, he was deeply depressed and so he continued for many days. In the New Year he was still reluctant to join the United States and France in introducing a currency for Western Europe. He was reluctant, yes, but when it was eventually introduced and the Russians blockaded Berlin, he was firmness itself in promoting the rescuing airlift. With immense resolution and ingenuity, he played a large part in the formation of the Atlantic Alliance, which has ever since provided the whole basis of Western defence against Soviet aggression.

I have never had the slightest doubt as to the justification of that policy of deterrence. The Atlantic Alliance was the indisputable step in 1947 if Western Europe was not to be overwhelmed. No one can seriously allege that since that time the Soviet Union has become less menacing or less expansionist. Angola, Ethiopia, South Yemen, Mozambique, Laos, Cambodia and South Vietnam have all been brought under Communist domination since 1974. Iran has been plunged into chaos and converted from a bastion of Western strength to a cauldron of virulent anti-Westernism, its oil treasures provocatively exposed to Russian eyes. Cuba acts increasingly as an agent of wide-ranging Soviet ambition. More recently we have witnessed the brutal conquest of Afghanistan and the latest phase of callous repression in Poland. If the Atlantic Alliance was an imperative defence against Soviet Russia when it was formed, the desperate need for it is still more obvious at the present moment.

At the end of 1980, when President Reagan was elected, it seemed likely that on existing trends the Soviet Union would be in a position by 1985 to dictate surrender terms to the USA and her allies. President Reagan has set out to correct the potential imbalance. I do not set out to pronounce on the respective military strength of the West and East nor on the wisdom or otherwise of the precise tactics being pursued, for example, by President Reagan. I am concerned with the fundamental moral issue. The pacifist option will always remain open to a Christian. Unless one is a Christian pacifist, which I am not, the policy of deterrence remains for the Atlantic allies the one clear means of fulfilling their Christian obligation.

That cannot be the last word about a situation fraught with such possibilities of unlimited harm. Someone of my age is, perhaps, too much inclined to see the present argument about nuclear weapons as a logical continuation of the ancient debate between pacifists and non-pacifists. But there are many Christians, including those more elevated in the Churches than I am, who are convinced that a new dimension has been added to the argument by the invention of weapons which could literally obliterate the world. My mind lingers too much, they will tell me, on the pre-war debates when a pacifist Christian would pose the question: "Can you imagine Christ in a bomber plane?" and be met with the retort: "Can you imagine Christ in plus fours?"

Is the Christian tradition of the just war still relevant?

Just-war thinking does not seek to legitimise, and still less to glorify, war. It recognises, however, that recourse to armed force cannot rationally be regarded as unjustifiable in all circumstances. The war must be undertaken and waged exclusively by the leaders of the State. War must be fought for a just cause. Recourse to war must be a last resort. There should be a formal declaration of war. Those engaging in war must have a reasonable hope of success. The evil and damage which the war entails must be judged to be proportionate to the injury it is designed to avert, or the injustice which occasioned it. If these conditions are satisfied, it is morally licit to resort to war. The means must be suited to the objective and must be just and honourable. The two principles of "non-combatant immunity" and "proportion" give some guidance in the matter.

To quote from *The Church and the Bomb* again:

> What is required is that any method of warfare be consonant with the lawful aim of the war and also that it be acceptable to a person of upright conscience, for the upright conscience is the measure of moral acceptability. An upright conscience is one formed by a lifelong habit of love, generosity, mercy, justice, courage, patience and all other virtues.

In the end all these profound considerations have to be brought together in a practical judgment. The Pope told the United Nations in June 1982 that "under present circumstances deterrence based on balance, not as an end in itself but as a step on the way to progressive disarmament, may still be judged as morally acceptable."

Christians, in so far as they respect the Pope's authority, are entitled to pursue policies broadly similar to those pursued at present by the Atlantic powers. But that can only be part of the truth, as I and other Christians have argued before now in the House of Lords. Christians would be betraying their religion if they did not redouble their exertions in pursuit of multilateral nuclear – and indeed all forms – of disarmament.

Since 1945 there have been many wars, some of them still in progress. It seems, however, impossible to omit all mention of the war in the Falklands, where acute problems were raised for British Christians. In the summer of 1982 the old problem of rendering unto Caesar the things that are Caesar's and unto God the things that are God's presented itself sharply when the Falklands crisis coincided with the Pope's visit to England. Before he came to England he had begged both parties to the dispute to accept a ceasefire. Leading churchmen from Britain and the Argentine had met in Rome. The Pope's request was turned down flatly by the British Government, although it was made plain to him that it was very much hoped that his visit would proceed.

Some of us listened to his impassioned plea for peace in Westminster Cathedral. There seemed a painful conflict between his spiritual objectives and the determination of the British Government to carry through the war to a successful conclusion by steps taken almost at the same time.

The great majority of the British people seemed to feel no contradiction between his heartfelt prayers for peace and an uninhibited victorious campaign. They must be deemed to have felt that peace with justice and honour could only be restored by a British reconquest of the Falklands.

Can we then, returning to our original question, talk of a Christian attitude to war? For Christians Christ will always be the Prince of Peace. Christians hate war; so does everyone not bereft of his senses. But Christians, as explained elsewhere in this book, provide a doctrine of forgiveness which is indeed distinctive. This makes reconciliation a moral necessity when the guns cease firing. That emphasis was very evident in the Thanksgiving Service which followed the war in the Falklands. The Churches insisted on it to their eternal credit.

In the Falklands themselves, a profoundly moving ser-

vice was organised for the relatives of the British service-
men who died there. The chaplain-general to the forces
included in his address these memorable words: "We come
with pride, not the pride of boastfulness or conceit, nor the
pride of the victor over the vanquished. We remember
another Christian place not far from here where are buried
many young men." He was referring to the Argentine dead
lying over the hill.

One must be grateful for the Christian leadership on this
occasion. It was less potent at the end of the Second World
War. There were many signs of a spirit of reconciliation
among Christians, though not only among Christians. But
the national mood after six years of war was not at first
forgiving. The official British attitude, not different from
that of her allies, was shared alike by Conservatives and
socialists with relatively few exceptions. Germany, it was
agreed, must be held down, her industry must be dis-
mantled, she must be occupied for many years to come.
I myself, the Minister – as already mentioned – for the British zone, said to a high Foreign Office official about prop-
osed pension arrangements for the British Control Commission: "You seem to be assuming that we shall be here
for at least twenty-five years." He replied without hesita-
tion: "I should be most sorry not to think so."

In the event, the behaviour of the Soviet Union produced a totally different attitude to Germany within a few
years. Germany was welcomed back as an equal and
essential partner in the defence of the West against the
Soviet menace. All that was on the plane of diplomacy and
secular prudence. But there was another inspiration, totally opposed to the Potsdam settlement, in which Christians
provided an honourable leadership.

The men I have particularly in mind – I could mention
plenty of others at all levels – were the Bishop of Chiches-
ter George Bell, Dick Stokes the Catholic MP, and Victor
Gollancz. The latter, though a Jew, was at that time
propounding Christian values more passionately and elo-

quently than anyone in public affairs. Within the Control Commission, youngish men like Alec Bishop, regional commissioner of North Rhine-Westphalia, and Robert Birley, chief educational advisor, brought to the new Germany the best that "old England" could offer.

Sometimes, as here, ideas of reconciliation and forgiveness, which do not usually figure in the political programme, outlast worldly calculations and provide – even by worldly standards – the truest wisdom.

11   Christianity and Ireland

In 1983, the view was not infrequently expressed in England that "if this is what religion does to Ireland, a country would be better off without it." The whole world has been made aware of the horrifying violence in the North of Ireland since 1969. To take one figure, which happens to be in front of me: in the five years 1977–1982, 400 men were convicted of terrorist murder in the North of Ireland. In certain parts of the province, there has been a state of guerrilla warfare.

Who is to blame? Everyone will answer that question in the light of their own experience. I hope to be forgiven if I spend a little time in describing mine.

I have said earlier that I have always been proud to be Irish. I have mentioned the influence of my brother and Mr. de Valera in causing me to become an Irish nationalist. As a small boy with a romantic family home in Ireland, I was always Irish in my own eyes, just as, no doubt, Lord Home was Scottish in his. From 1922, when I was sixteen, the parallelism could not be exact. I was from then on a member of two states – the United Kingdom and the Irish Free State. When I grew up I was entitled to two passports. For some years I used an Irish one. However, in 1947 I became British Minister for Germany, making frequent visits to that country. I was persuaded by "the security boys" that it was injudicious for a British minister to use a non-British passport.

Soon afterwards, Ireland became a republic outside the Commonwealth, technically a foreign country. Through it all for nearly sixty years, I have shouted for Ireland at the international rugby matches at Twickenham and Lansdowne Road. Several times I visited the latter with President de Valera. He was always considerate towards my supposedly mixed feelings. On one occasion we learnt from the loudspeaker at half time that France had beaten England in Paris. There was a good deal of jocular cheering. "These old antagonisms die hard," murmured Mr. de Valera consolingly. Many other aspects of my dual allegiance were developed by me in a lecture in Dublin entitled "Double Agent".

For eight years I was chairman of the National Bank (now merged) which then had headquarters in London and some branches in England, but many more in Ireland, including some in the North. In 1935 I published my *Peace by Ordeal*, which has become the standard history of the Anglo–Irish treaty of 1921; in 1970, I published with Tom O'Neill an authorised *Life of Eamon de Valera* and, in 1981 with Anne McHardie, *Ulster*.

My family – until I went over – had always been Protestant, except that my great-uncle, a young Guards officer called Reginald Charles, became Father Paul-Mary, a Passionist monk who took that Order to Ireland. It was to him that his uncle, the Duke of Wellington, addressed the soldierly instruction: "Well, Charles, you have been a good soldier. Strive to be a good monk."

My book *Peace by Ordeal* was published about five years before I became a Catholic, but I certainly felt close to Mr. de Valera in an instinctive Christianity. The book played a small part in securing a new recognition for him among his opponents.

The inevitability of Irish neutrality was recognised by most of the British leaders during the Second World War, though not by Winston Churchill. He was to show his respect for Mr. de Valera in later years. He would refer to southern Ireland as "an independent, Christian, cultured, law-respecting" state.

Over the whole period 1922–1983, the twenty-six counties of southern Ireland have been vastly more successful than most people in Britain expected. There has been, in spite of acute economic problems at the time of writing, a marked improvement in the standard of living, which has brought Ireland much closer to the British level. In spite of the outburst of violence in the North, the Irish Republic has been exceptionally law-abiding. There has been far less crime in Ireland, even in urban districts, than in Great Britain. There has been no decline in morals of the kind associated with a permissive society throughout the Western world, though the Irish social code, springing from a rather old-fashioned Catholicism and excluding, for example, divorce, would not be acceptable in Britain.

Religion is still a tremendous force. Eighty-five per cent of the population still go to church every Sunday. Anyone who joined the vast crowds applauding the Pope on his visit in 1979 will be aware that religion and patriotism are still inextricably interwoven. The Pope had a wonderful reception when he visited England and Scotland in 1982, but there could not be the same depth of response in a country predominantly Protestant or non-believing.

Once more, who is to blame? The first answer given will be "the terrorists, Catholic and Protestant". That answer cannot be lightly set aside. I heard the Pope say, in memorable terms, on his visit to Northern Ireland: "Murder is murder." Nothing said below must be taken to whittle down that condemnation. I sat between Lord Mountbatten and his son-in-law, Lord Brabourne, not long before the first was assassinated, and the second barely survived. Two small boys were murdered along with Lord Mountbatten. But in Northern Ireland before the Troubles, there was in the South far less crime than in England. The Northern Ireland community has not suddenly turned into a people of villains. We must look deeper and seek causes.

The historical fact is that the Irish Protestants, though in a minority of one to three-and-a-half in the whole island, are in a majority of two to one in the Six Counties. They have at all times been supported by British governments for their own reasons, in pursuing a policy of discrimination against the Catholics. In recent years, the United Kingdom has tried to secure better treatment for the Catholics in the North.

But little progress has been made to undo the lamentable legacy of past centuries. In England, Scotland and Wales, and other parts of the world, Catholics and Protestants live and work together in amity. So many of them do in Northern Ireland, but the sectarian traditions remain dominant there.

In Southern Ireland, the relationship, admittedly under totally different circumstances, is today on the whole satisfactory. There was more tension when I was a boy. Tales of old-time bigotry were still handed on with amusement. We ourselves, though Protestant, happened to live among Catholic neighbours. The mother of the children we knew best was a Protestant who married a Catholic. She had received a telegram on her wedding day at the church: "Your mother's curse certain; your father's probable. (He was dead.) Not a good beginning for married life."

Many years later, in 1961, when my brother died, I went over to Dublin for the funeral service performed by the Protestant Archbishop of Dublin. My brother had been made a senator by Mr. de Valera; a minute's silence was observed for him in the Dublin theatres, to which he had devoted his life. An immense crowd gathered at the graveside. But no Catholics, except his family and some "irregulars" like Brendan Behan, ventured into the church. A few years later, following the Vatican Council, this would have been inconceivable, as the Archbishop of Dublin told me. I only mention it now to show that I am aware that there was plenty of bigotry in the Catholic Church, a point never to be overlooked by Catholics when criticising the bigotry of Protestants.

Be all that as it may, it was generally reckoned that

Catholics and Protestants could not live and work together in a Northern government. From 1969 I myself was advocating what came to be known as "power sharing" – a government that would include those from the Catholic minority. In 1974, the experiment was tried and was succeeding. It was sabotaged by the Ulster workers' strike. Nothing remained except the demonstration that what had happened once could be achieved again.

On paper, the conditions now are much more propitious than they have ever been. There is no British defence interest left in Ireland, except one of reasonable stability. The EEC is bringing together both parts of Ireland and the United Kingdom in a wider context. Most important of all, the world-wide ecumenical movement has led the leaders – and, to some extent, the lower clergy of all the churches (except the independent Presbyterians) – to behave towards each other in the manner expected of Christians. There is no limit to the number of noble-minded voluntary initiatives. Yet, at the time of writing, there is total deadlock. There is no sign of political progress.

My own summary would be this: the cursed religious wars of the seventeenth century have left their tragic mark on Northern Ireland. But if Christianity means what it claims to mean, and what I believe it to mean, the evil left behind by a distorted religion will one day be undone by a religion altogether closer to the spirit of Christ.

PART FOUR

Renewal

Renewal

Christians believe in a loving God. Christians hold the conviction that in some future state of being, in the words of Julian of Norwich, "All will be well, and all manner of things will be well." Such a belief is integral to a religious attitude. But so is an equally strong conviction that it is a sin against the Holy Ghost (though not the one referred to in the Gospels) to fold one's hands and leave the future to God. In other words, faith and works are equally necessary.

Such a religious attitude does not in itself determine our optimism or pessimism about life on this planet. My great friend Malcolm Muggeridge, for example, is gloomy enough about the prospects here below; he rests happy and confident in a secure and unshakeable belief in God's mercy. I myself, committed for so many years to active politics, social reform and social work, have developed occupationally a secular optimism which is probably rather firmer than is warranted by a close study of the facts.

I have tried to look at these matters dispassionately. There are vast areas of life which cannot be measured or weighed up quantitatively; but where measurement is possible the facts are grim, and getting, on the whole, grimmer.

We can distinguish various forms of crisis, real or alleged. There is first the moral area: crime, the family, sex and religion. On the face of it there is little for our comfort here. The crime figures go up and up, and the Home Office seems to be assuming that in a few years' time they will be even higher. (I am referring to Britain but the experience is general.) Along with the increase in crime, and no doubt deriving from it, the general attitude towards criminals has become less and less Christian.

No one can dispute the widespread loosening of sexual morals in Britain and other Western countries. There can be no shutting one's eyes to the horrifying figures for the increase of divorce, illegitimacy and abortion. In regard to these, as in regard to pornography, the permissive society has much to answer for in recent years. In each case some counter-attack is in progress. There is no cause for premature optimism but, as always, despair is the one deadly sin.

However, I must not leave the impression that the most enlightened Christians are adopting a purely negative posture – trying to put the clock back, without any sense of remorse for not having done more to help the lost sheep. There is no better guide in this field than Dr. Jack Cominian, Catholic psychiatrist, who writes as follows:

> . . . The disciplines of psychology and psychoanalysis are showing categorically that sex is a most powerful means of constructing, maintaining and reinforcing human bonds of affection and love . . . Christianity has now to proclaim unequivocally the joy and goodness of sexuality to an age that longs to experience it but is confused.

He restates the old principles, though always places them in the context of widening and deepening the meaning of love. We seem here to be at the beginning of wisdom.

It is easy, in fact habitual in many quarters, to talk of a steady decline in religion. I often ask those who make such pronouncements to name a Golden Age when this country was much more religious than it is now. I have never been given a convincing answer. But it is beyond dispute that there has been a marked decline in church-going and church membership in twentieth-century Britain.

Dr. Alan Gilbert – in his powerful, if over-dogmatic,

book *The Making of Post-Christian Britain* – provides some illustrations:

> In the single decade of the 1960s . . . Episcopalian Easter Day communicants fell by 24.5 per cent in England, 32 per cent in Wales and 12 per cent in Scotland. The Church of Scotland actually ceased to count active communicants as early as 1959, but the splinter organisation, the United Free Church of Scotland, saw it decline by 26 per cent in the decade. In England, Presbyterian active communicants were 17 per cent fewer in 1970 than they had been ten years earlier. Figures on membership, a more sluggish index, showed a 15 per cent decline in Methodism, a 22 per cent decline in Congregational-ism and a 13 per cent decline in Baptist strength in the 1960s. The most recent figures indicate that the 1970s have brought no substantial reversal of this trend, and have seen it accelerate in some Churches.

The crucial question is, however, whether religion has really declined, or whether the changes have been, in Dr. Gilbert's words, "confined to various external manifesta-tions of an otherwise unabated religious impulse".

No one possesses, or is likely to possess, the data on which to measure the amount of religious belief at any one moment. The secrets of the human heart are not accessible to the statistician, but common sense suggests that some decline in belief must have gone hand in hand with the decline in church attendance. A nation that seldom goes to church will almost certainly be less influenced by religion than one that goes to church regularly.

The question of whether moral conduct has deteriorated correspondingly is separate again. Northern Ireland, a strongly church-going community, has been afflicted by so many political factors that the strong religious influence, which takes a sectarian form, cannot easily be correlated with moral behaviour. The fact of the decline in religious influence in Britain is hard to challenge, although the trend is not irreversible.

There are, however, straws in the wind which point the other way. The unparalleled enthusiasm for the papal visit to this Protestant country was a new demonstration that Christianity is nothing like as peripheral as Dr. Gilbert supposes. Mrs. Thatcher's urgent desire that the Pope's visit should not be cancelled, even though she turned down his plea for a cease-fire over the Falklands, suggests that Christianity is a national influence that the wisest politicians are fully aware of. The heated arguments about the proper character of the Falklands Thanksgiving Service demonstrated more clearly than for many years the major role of the Christian leaders in our public life.

Dr. Gilbert finds the best hope for a religious revival in a kind of evangelical sectarianism. For myself, I find it in the ever more notable developments of the ecumenical movement. Dr. Runcie has left us in no doubt that complete Christian unity is his goal.

The issues cannot be disposed of by simple labels. Some years ago in the House of Lords, Lord Alexander of Hillsbrough, leader of the Labour peers, a staunch Baptist and opponent of everything that smacked of popery, listened with approval to a Catholic peer who was delivering a harangue in favour of old-fashioned morality. Lord Alexander turned to a fellow Nonconformist, the ex-miner Lord Lawson, and with me sitting on the other side of him commented: "You know, Jack, these Catholics will soon be the only nonconformists left."

In my eyes the progress towards Christian unity, far greater than I would ever have expected twenty years ago, represents by far the most encouraging development of recent years.

In the international sphere, the West has found no way of reaching the kind of reconciliation with Soviet Russia that would make possible even a limited measure of disarmament. The arms race continues apace, conjuring up unbearable nightmares for anyone with a trace of imagination. Nevertheless the possibility of a world calamity is so horrendous that the attempts to secure multilateral disarmament must be desperately accelerated.

I turn briefly to economics. The whole situation is sufficiently macabre at a time when the steady advance in science should be raising the standard of living year after year. Western capitalism is certainly putting up what my old chief, Sir William Beveridge, would have called a "miserable show". It is poor consolation that Communism should be faring even worse.

Regeneration must begin on the moral plane. But, of course, it cannot end there. A moral revival does not automatically endow us with inspiring leaders, intelligent economic theories, a spirit of business enterprise or far-sighted diplomacy. In my lifetime Lloyd George and John Maynard Keynes – and, going a hundred years further back, the great diplomatist Talleyrand – rendered permanent service to humanity, but I would not say that any of these people provided a moral message; a message, I mean, that led to human beings behaving better to one another. Of course, every country, at all times, will require political and social policies and programmes. The respective merits of inflation and deflation will never cease to be canvassed. Ernest Bevin once said to me, "Inflation is making a successful speech at a public dinner – deflation is waking up your wife to tell her about it." I am not sure that we have any better definitions at the present time.

I lay great emphasis on the distinction between a just society on paper, and the revolution in moral outlook which is indispensable if it is to achieve its purpose. Can we hope to find such moral inspiration in any kind of Marxism? Not surprisingly, as a Christian, I am satisfied that Marxism, with its atheistic materialist philosophy, is not the answer. Today I find many young people on the left, including Communists, Trotskyites and Militants, who boldly claim to be Marxists without having read Marx. Yet no one but a fool would deny the extent of his contemporary influence.

This bearded old Victorian, who laboured away in the British Museum a few yards from where I work, has had more influence on human lives than any individual since Jesus Christ, with the possible exception of Mohammed; that is, if you measure his achievement by the number of people who are, nominally at least, carrying out his theories. One thing can be said: where Marxism is held to have succeeded it has been associated hitherto with totalitarianism, or dictatorship, and few of us suppose that this is the right solution for Britain, or the West in general.

At this point morals and economics overlap. Some years ago the then Archbishop of Canterbury, Dr. Coggan, singled out greed as the prevailing vice of our time. I would hesitate to argue that personal greed in the materialist sense has increased in recent years, but collective greed is much better organised, and much more pernicious. This is equally true whether we are talking of businessmen, professional people or trade unionists. It is fair to the last-named to say that the example was set to them many years ago from the top. Our textbooks taught us that "economic man" was the mainspring of society, and "economic man" is another name for "greedy man". For a long time the working classes were in no position to follow this model, but in recent years they have copied their "betters" and applied the lesson all too well.

No one is better qualified to speak as a Christian socialist than Frank Field MP, who has done more for the poor and for the principles of equality than any other single individual. The Child Poverty Action Group, with which he will always be identified, has been one of the most impressive lobbies of our time. Frank Field accepts the well-known dictum that the Labour Party owed more in the past to Methodism than to Marxism, but he reluctantly admits that this is no longer so.

This change in the basis of the authority for the Party's beliefs goes some way to explain the long-term decline in the Party's support. Field considers, however, that the emphasis on the Methodist heritage has led to an underestimation of that which has come from Anglicanism. Here the influence was not so much in the equipping of individuals for public roles, as occurred with the training of Methodist lay preachers. It built up rather a theology which, by stressing the Incarnation, took redemption away from an almost laissez-faire, individualistic relationship with God, to one stressing the importance to God of all that happens in this world and the prospect of general redemption.

This Anglican theology, by developing the sense of a collective as well as an individualistic wish to do good, played a crucial part in developing a political atmosphere conducive to the acceptance and growth of Labour politics.

What is sadly lacking today on the left is any such theological tradition. Frank Field considers that any discussion of the redemption of the West necessarily turns, for a Christian, on the Church's recovery of its prophetic and teaching role.

Such a recovery will spill over into the political arena, for it will be through political actions that a collective redemption is achieved. All this can be subscribed to by Free Churchmen and Catholics as well as Anglicans. But even if all goes well, it will be a long haul. It is not possible to be inspired by a brilliant vacuum or question mark.

During the Falklands crisis, which coincided with the Pope's visit to Britain, I met a lady of Conservative background who had long experience of social work. I asked her, "Where do you look today for leadership?" She replied, though not herself a Catholic, "To the Pope." I persisted, and she answered just as positively, "To Mrs. Thatcher." Let us for a moment look carefully at the messages of the Pope and Mrs. Thatcher, taking Mrs. Thatcher first.

Mrs. Thatcher's philosophy and politics matter even more than would usually be the case in a prime minister, for two reasons. In the first place, no prime minister in this century has dominated a Cabinet in peacetime in her special fashion. One has to go back to Gladstone, or before him to Robert Peel, for comparison; and in those days the areas of life covered by government policies were much smaller. In the second place, her policies represent a far more drastic break with the past, including the immediate past of her own party, than any since the Labour rule of 1945–51, when after a world war far-reaching changes were generally expected.

Indeed, there is a third reason why Margaret Thatcher is specially significant even among prime ministers. She must be described (in a complimentary rather than a pejorative sense) as a moralist politician, the first of that kind since Gladstone. I take for granted her private life, which is exemplary, like that of all our leaders as far as we can tell since Lloyd George, who had other merits. I am suggesting, however, that Mrs. Thatcher is a preacher of morals. She is deliberately setting out to improve the moral standards of this country by exhortation and, where possible, by government action. It goes without saying that no more than in the case of Gladstone are her political opponents prepared to accept her sermons as inspired text.

She has for some years, and long before the Falklands crisis, called for a return to the ancient virtues of self-help, self-discipline and self-sacrifice. No one questions her own powers of self-help and self-discipline, and anyone who renounces, as she has done, a quarter of her salary must be listened to with respect on the subject of self-sacrifice. But when her moral convictions lead her into the field of social morality they become extremely controversial. She leaves a clear impression that she considers that the principle of self-sacrifice has been undervalued for many years; that our attempts to be our brother's keeper have dragged down both our brother and ourselves into the pit; that the Welfare State in Britain has been carried forward too far and too fast.

Many of us consider that one example of the decline of Britain in recent years is our failure to develop our welfare provision, in which we were the pioneers, as fully as a number of European countries have done. Those who think like Mrs. Thatcher would probably believe exactly the opposite. We like to feel that in this country, compared with before the war, we have created a compassionate society. Mrs. Thatcher herself on becoming prime minister quoted at 10 Downing Street St Francis of Assisi's prayer for peace. We cannot equate St Francis of Assisi with over three million unemployed. When Mr. Norman St John-Stevas, the Leader of the House of Commons, was dismissed from the Cabinet, he pointed out the contrast between the caring Conservatism which he stood for and the actual policies of the Government.

Peregrine Worsthorne is ready to accept his role as a lone voice among intellectuals, but he has pointed to the extraordinary improvement of the standing of the Government, and Mrs. Thatcher in particular, since the short, successful war over the Falklands to justify his claim that it is she who, in these last years, speaks for the people. How, he cries out rhetorically, could so many writers live through this period without sensing the almost tangible resurrection of Britain as a moral force, as a community with a proud idea of itself, for which individuals were prepared to die? For many ordinary people the conflict was an ennobling experience, even a religious one, transcending anything which they had ever felt before. "For the first time," wrote Peregrine Worsthorne, "they were conscious of belonging to something larger than themselves – other than a football club – something greater and immeasurably more significant."

Time alone will show whether this new sense of national identity, real or alleged, will have any effect on conduct and thus play a part in the desired resurrection of Britain. At this stage I postulate only that a scheme of things depending on the restoration of the ancient virtues will achieve nothing, or less than nothing, unless it preserves and enhances the new humanity which many of us feel has been the redeeming feature of a post-war Britain in which so much else has gone wrong.

In 1983 Mrs. Thatcher won an overwhelming victory at the general election. She is entitled to take full credit. It has certainly been a remarkable exhibition of character, but the questions posed above remain.

We have heard at different times about various kinds of society – the "permissive society", the "civilised society", the "compassionate society" to name only three. My own label (not Mrs. Thatcher's) for her ideal society would be the "deserving society". The England she would like to see is one where everyone is rewarded according to their merits. Everyone, that is, except those so afflicted, avoidably or unavoidably, that they need special assistance. She assumes that the vast majority of us will benefit by feeling, "It's up to me, not the State." She believes that this will make us better people and will produce a better country. Many Christians, however, will continue to seek a programme closer to the spirit of her favourite saint, St Francis.

The Pope's visit to Britain was an unqualified success. The Catholics of this country were enormously strengthened, but his impact extended far beyond his own communion. The ecumenical cause, the hope of Christian unity, has been furthered immensely. Here one does not wish to give more credit to the Pope than to the Archbishop of Canterbury. Clifford Longley, himself a Catholic, called the service in Canterbury Cathedral, in which the Archbishop of Canterbury and the Pope both participated and gave addresses, "an Anglican triumph". That seems to me the essential truth. The Pope behaved, as he does on all occasions, with extreme charm and sensitivity, but it was the Church of England, and particularly Archbishop Runcie, who made it an historic victory.

Archbishop Runcie said:

Our unity is not in the past only, but also in the future . . . If we remember that beginning in Jesus Christ Our Lord, if we can lift our eyes beyond the historic quarrels which have tragically disfigured Christ's Church and wasted so much Christian energy, then we shall indeed enter into a faith worthy of celebration because it is able to remake the world.

He has been giving a powerful and positive lead towards Christian unity, and his speech and entire bearing through-out the service set the seal on his exertions.

My mind goes back twenty years to the time when Archbishop (later Lord) Fisher took the brave step of visiting the Pope in Rome. I knew him quite well from the House of Lords, and had some idea of what it must have cost him in his relations with some of his communion. But having once put his hand to the plough he waxed bolder and bolder. In a debate in the House of Lords on Christian unity, he was repeatedly interrogated by the militant Baptist Lord Alexander, Leader of the Opposition. Finally Lord Alexander called out in exasperation: "Well, which is the Church of England, anyway, Protestant or Catholic?" To which Archbishop Fisher replied, his eyes dancing with fun, "Both." Lord Alexander was temporarily subdued, but he came back later and was soon demonstrating to me, once again, that the phrase in Hebrews, "a sacrifice not to be repeated", invalidated any kind of Mass – Anglican or Roman Catholic. There has been, indeed, wonderful progress since that time. It has represented in my eyes the most glorious feature of recent world history.

The Pope spoke on the theme of unity, taking as his text John 17. Sermons without number have been delivered on that basis, but the Pope spoke about love with unique authority. Afterwards a common declaration was published, from which this sentence stands out: "Our aim is not limited to the union of our two communions alone to the exclusion of other Christians, but rather extends to the fulfilment of God's will for the visible unity of all his people."

I am not in any very orthodox sense a believer in the

personal devil, but I find it easy to place myself in his situation, and survey the struggle between belief and unbelief from his angle. The progress towards Christian unity, inconceivable when I became a Catholic forty years ago, is the worst news for the devil since the Reformation. It is consoling to be able to point to one large area where progress has already exceeded our dreams, and where there seems no limit to what can be accomplished by the end of the century.

But, leaving out the ecumenical aspect of the Pope's visit, what will be the moral effect of his various pronouncements on the British people as a whole?

If one could consider only one of his public appearances, one might select the service at Southwark Cathedral, where his subject was the anointing of the sick. No written description can do justice to the personal love for the handicapped of which he gave practical illustration. I was not unprepared for this, having seen him bending over wheelchairs at Knock in Western Ireland, and in Rome. What he said to the handicapped at Southwark was glorious: "You will find the crucified Lord in the midst of your sickness and suffering." Of even wider appeal was what he called his "urgent plea" to this nation:

> Do not neglect your sick and elderly. Do not turn away from the handicapped and the dying. Do not push them to the margins of society. For if you do, you will fail to see that they represent an important truth. The sick, the elderly, the handicapped and the dying teach us that weakness is a creative part of human living and that suffering can be embraced with no loss of dignity. Let us keep the sick and the handicapped at the centre of our lives. Let us treasure them and recognise with gratitude the debt we owe them. We begin by imagining that we are giving to them, we end by realising that they have enriched us.

The inspiration that he expressed in word and deed on this occasion is no monopoly of popes, or of Catholics, or even of Christians. It is, in a thousand different forms, the legacy of the British and of other humane peoples, but when I heard those words of his, and later learned of the public reaction, I realised the almost unlimited desire to help their fellow men which is half-stifled in the British and other Western peoples. If we suffer from any special contemporary weakness, it is the insistence on our own rights to the exclusion of our own duties. What H. A. L. Fisher, the historian, called the "liberal experiment" of the last two centuries has culminated in an assertion of personal freedom and the right to still more freedom. But once our hearts are touched we make a new calculation – or rather cease to make one at all.

I assume that altruism is part of our God-given nature, but that it is engaged in unending strife with selfishness. The moral ambiguity of the West will continue until a sufficient number of men and women decide to put service before self. And why should this process not begin in Britain, where the tradition of service has at various times provided an inspiring example to the world? Can this noble vision be realised without religion, which in Britain largely means Christianity? It is not, in my conviction, likely.

I am thinking ultimately of the liberation of the human spirit, the one sure pathway to Christ. Without religion, freedom is at the external mercy of the devilish powers with which in this century we are only too well acquainted. Without religion, freedom is at the internal mercy of the group selfishness, identified truly as the curse of our Western community. To quote Archbishop William Temple, theologian, philosopher and spiritual leader, speaking many years ago in my hearing at the Oxford Union:

> Only religious faith can make the world safe for freedom,
> Only religious faith can make freedom safe for the world.